Exploring
Museum Theatre

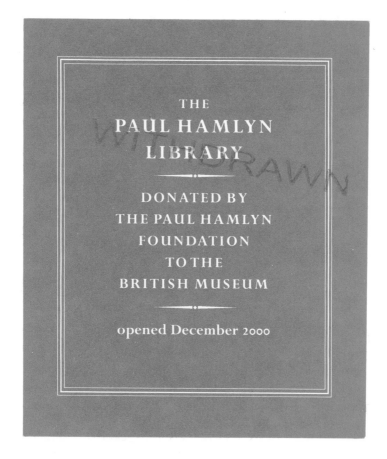

Exploring Museum Theatre

TESSA BRIDAL

A Division of
ROWMAN & LITTLEFIELD PUBLISHERS, INC.
Walnut Creek • *Lanham* • *New York* • *Toronto* • *Oxford*

If facts are the seeds from which
knowledge grows, then the
emotions and the impressions of
the senses are the fertile soil in
which these seeds must grow . . .
It is not half so important to
know, as to feel. —Rachel Carson, *A Sense of Wonder*

AltaMira Press
A division of Rowman & Littlefield Publishers, Inc.
1630 North Main Street, #367
Walnut Creek, California 94596
www.altamirapress.com

Rowman & Littlefield Publishers, Inc.
A wholly owned subsidiary of The Rowman & Littlefield Publishing Group, Inc.
4501 Forbes Boulevard, Suite 200
Lanham, Maryland 20706

PO Box 317
Oxford
OX2 9RU, UK

British Library Cataloguing in Publication Information Available

Library of Congress Cataloging-in-Publication Data

Bridal, Tessa, 1947–
    Exploring museum theatre / Tessa Bridal.
        p. cm. — (American association for state and local history book series)
    Includes bibliographical references (p.   ) and index.
    ISBN 0-7591-0412-3 (hardcover : alk. paper) — ISBN 0-7591-0413-1 (pbk. : alk.
paper)
    1. Museum theater. 2. Museums—Educational aspects. 3. Museum exhibits.
I. Title. II. Series.
AM7.B75 2004
069'.16—dc22   2004006866

Printed in the United States of America

∞™ The paper used in this publication meets the minimum requirements of American
National Standard for Information Sciences—Permanence of Paper for Printed Library
Materials, ANSI/NISO Z39.48-1992.

Contents

Preface, or
Dramatic Prologue

In bygone years theatre performances frequently included a chorus to provide commentary on the dramatic action, or a character fulfilling the duties of a guide and narrator. The current richness of museum theatre offers a wealth of such choruses and guides to choose from, and making them known to you is one of the goals of this book.

Another goal is to examine the term *museum theatre* and the many activities it has been used to describe, from formally staged productions to the use of mascots. My purpose is not to judge the theatrical merit of any of these efforts, but to assist practitioners in developing a common language with which to describe their particular activities, and clarify the terms used to promote them to audiences and to other practitioners. This common language will help us to focus and define our work and clearly convey our intentions to our audiences.

This book also reviews the history of museum theatre and its emergence from the ranks of educational theatre, and provides what it is fashionable to call a "tool box" in the form of various appendixes. Being a theatre buff, I will call it a "theatre trunk," where you will find sample budgets for museum theatre programs and productions, contracts, and job descriptions for theatre personnel.

To help me provide an overview of the current state of museum theatre, several museums, several historical sites, and a zoo generously consented to serve as examples of a variety of museum theatre practices. These organizations have made recognized contributions to the field of museum theatre, including the presentation and publication of the results of their work at conferences, workshops, and in professional journals; the development of theatrical performances in a variety of styles; and the creative use of personnel, including professional actors, education staff, volunteers, and youth. They are innovators in the use of spaces and styles, and they have demonstrated courage and leadership by presenting controversial topics, targeting underserved audiences, and mentoring others. They devoted many hours to answering a lengthy written questionnaire and to conversations with me. When quotes are not otherwise attributed (to a journal or other publication) they are from these questionnaires and interviews. Please join me in a round of applause for:

The Carnegie Museum of Natural History, Pittsburgh, Pennsylvania

Explora Children's Museum and Science Center, Albuquerque, New Mexico

The Frederick R. Weisman Art Museum, Minneapolis, Minnesota

The Lawrence Hall of Science, Berkeley, California

The Minnesota History Center, Saint Paul, Minnesota

The Museo de Historia Natural "Dr. Carlos A. Torres de la Llosa," Montevideo, Uruguay

The Philadelphia Zoo, Philadelphia, Pennsylvania

The Science Museum of Minnesota, St. Paul, Minnesota

The Science Museum of Virginia, Richmond, Virginia

The Wheaton History Center, Wheaton, Illinois

The Whitaker Center for Science and the Arts, Harrisburg, Pennsylvania

The Witte Museum, San Antonio, Texas

Special thanks are due to James L. Peterson, former director of the Science Museum of Minnesota, and to Anne Hornickel, director of Museum Programs there, both staunch advocates of live interpretation. I also want to acknowledge Stephanie Long, for her help in preparing the manuscript, and Ron Eyrich, for his inspired designs of the Science Live Theatre and the Atrium Stage. Current and former curators and exhibit hall directors have fought the good fight to preserve museum theatre programs at the Science Museum of Minnesota and deserve to be acknowledged—Lou Casagrande, Patrick Hamilton, John Newlin, and Orrin Shane. This book would not have been possible without the exceptional artistic freedom granted to me by the Science Museum of Minnesota, where I have been allowed to succeed and fail, to experiment, innovate, and teach.

My deep appreciation goes to the American Association for State and Local History's Publication Committee for their support of this book. Susan Walters at AltaMira Press gave generously of her expertise and encouragement throughout the process, and was always available to answer questions. Beth Luey of Arizona State University undertook the editing of the manuscript with understanding and grace. She helped me to focus on content and style, and the book is decidedly improved thanks to her efforts.

The work represented here contains the contributions of the dozens of multitalented and colorful museum and theatre professionals with whom it has been my privilege to work over the last twenty years. They have attended Theatre in Museums Workshops, written articles for the *Museum Theatre Journal* of the American Association of Museums' Museum Theatre Professional Interest Council (which it was my privilege to chair for almost a decade), and performed, designed, and written plays for me.

The eleven institutions most extensively and frequently quoted are briefly described below.

The Carnegie Museum of Natural History is part of a collective of four museums embodying the ideals of Pittsburgh industrialist Andrew Carnegie, who established the Carnegie Institute in 1895 to help people improve their lives through educational and cultural experiences. The Carnegie's theatre performances have mostly been presented as outreach to schools in Pennsylvania, West Virginia, and Ohio. Recently, some performances have also taken place in the museum itself for special events or at times of the year when there are large numbers of visitors. These performances have been in the lecture hall or on the exhibit floors. The Science on Stage program began at the Carnegie in the spring of 1995, when the company toured to ten schools in five Pennsylvania counties, reaching two thousand students. Six years later they were touring twenty-eight counties in Pennsylvania, West Virginia, and Ohio, reaching over fifty-three thousand students in 179 schools. The program has continued to grow.

Explora Science Center and Children's Museum of Albuquerque, New Mexico, began in the Albuquerque Children's Museum, which opened in March 1992 in a shopping mall, with five full-time employees and seven volunteers. Within a year, it had moved to a more spacious location, which included an enclosed area with carpet-covered stadium seating for forty to sixty people, called the Teaching Theatre. In 1995, the children's museum merged with the science center to become Explora Science Center and Children's Museum of Albuquerque. Its current visitorship is approximately sixty thousand people per year. In 2003 a permanent facility opened in the city's cultural campus near Old Town.

The Lawrence Hall of Science is located at the University of California, Berkeley, and it serves over half a million people each year with programs, exhibits, and materials at the intersection of science, mathematics and society, environmental issues, and public health concerns. The Lawrence Hall of Science is a pioneer in creating inquiry-driven, activity-based science and mathematics curriculum materials, used by approximately one in five students in the United States during their precollege education. The mission of the Science Discovery Theatre is to use a wide variety of theatre techniques to expand opportunities for learning. Since its inception in 1988, the Science Discovery Theatre has performed for over 620,000 students, parents, teachers, and community members throughout California. They offer workshops for at-risk youth, and the Teen Theatre program prepares teens to perform short plays for museum and peer audiences at schools.

The Minnesota History Center, home of the Minnesota Historical Society, opened in 1992, 150 years after the society was established. The center is a 427,000-square-foot building located in St. Paul containing a museum with more than 45,000 square feet of exhibit space. It also features a library where patrons can access books, state archives, manuscripts collections, audiovisual collections, and three-dimensional museum collections. Admission is free, and over three hundred thousand people visit each year. The center's interpretive goals are to "encourage choice and personal involvement, to convey a sense of ownership, and to help visitors see themselves not simply as reflected in the events of history but as indispensable tellers of the tale." Most of the History Center's theatre programs serve general museum audiences and are integrated into the overall design and interpretation of selected exhibits.

The Museo de Historia Natural "Dr. Carlos A. Torres de la Llosa" in Montevideo, Uruguay, was inaugurated in 1920 by the University of the Republic and in 1924 came under the jurisdiction of the Council of Secondary Education. It exhibits natural history collections acquired over eight decades by professors and students. It is the first museum in Latin America to experiment with the use of theatre. The program began in May 1999 with a six-day theatre workshop offered to representatives from various museums, and to teachers from all over the country. A team of teachers with experience in Montevideo's highly respected network of independent theatres was formed to develop, write, and perform the first play, ¿Cardenal amarillo donde estás? (Where Are You, Yellow Cardinal?). From October to December 2000, thirty-one performances took place for eight hundred preschoolers from both public and private schools. The play was followed in 2001 with a dramatization of Horacio Quiroga's short story A la deriva (Adrift) for high school audiences. The story covers the journey taken by a man dying of a snakebite downriver through the jungle. Twenty-two performances were offered for six hundred high schoolers, accompanied by a tour of the museum's snake exhibit and a live snake demonstration. The museum offered a second workshop in 2002, and in 2003 presented their newest production, a play about AIDS.

The Philadelphia Zoo Treehouse began in 1985, when the zoo's historic Antelope House, built in 1874, was renovated into an attraction for children, with six large fiberglass habitats in which children can play and pretend to be animals. The six habitats include a dinosaur swamp, the Everglades, a giant honeycomb, a milkweed meadow, a beaver pond, and a giant rainforest ficus tree. In 1987 a full-time theatre staff of three became part of the institution's general operating budget. Treehouse performers teach, host birthday parties that include a Treehouse show, and take the shows to schools. In 1991, the Treehouse began its popular overnight program Night Flight. Night Flight has hosted up to sixty-five hundred participants and generated over a quarter of a million dollars per year, maintaining a nearly 60 percent net profit. The zoo draws over a million visitors each year.

The Science Museum of Minnesota (SMM—due to frequent references this abbreviation will be used throughout the book) got its start in 1907. Its forerunner was the Saint Paul Academy of Natural Sciences, founded in 1870. In 1978 a new building and omnitheater were completed. As detailed by Inez Roach, in her epilogue to *A History of the Science Museum of Minnesota, 1907–1975,* "one of the unique features of the new Science Museum is its almost total use of theater techniques in exhibit construction, lighting, and programs. The entire exhibit department now consists of theater-trained people. . . . The museum's educational programs have also been planned for and executed by theater-trained staff. Sondra Quinn led the museum's educational department in creating audience participation programs." In 1999 the museum completed construction of a new and expanded facility on the Mississippi River.

SMM employs a professional director and actors on a salaried, full-time basis. Playwrights, designers, and technicians are contracted. Plays and demonstrations, both of which are performed by actors, are presented five days a week, between four and eight times a day. The museum has one enclosed, formal theatre space, the Science Live Theatre, which seats one hundred people. A second performance space, the Atrium Stage, has an enclosed backstage area and a small stage, located in the middle of a public area facing a café. Bench seating is provided. Performances also take place within various exhibit areas.

The Science Museum of Virginia has over two hundred interactive exhibits and offers several lecture series, numerous on-site and outreach educational programs, and a wide variety of public events. Its Carpenter Science Theatre Company was conceived of in 1995 by Barry Hayes, and funded a year later by a $160,000 grant from the E. Rhodes and Leona B. Carpenter Foundation. The company began with a "MainStage" production. This was a full-length, two-act play, *Playing with Fire,* which questioned the ethics of unrestrained experimentation. It was followed by a series of short "OnStage" gallery shows. Performances also took place at two satellite museums, the Virginia Aviation Museum and the Danville Science Center. In 1998, the company received another $120,000 grant from the foundation. The performance schedule expanded to three to five days a week, and a full-time artistic director was hired to direct and perform with the company. In 2000, the foundation funded the Carpenter Science Theatre Company with a third grant, of $500,000 this time, and theatre attendance increased by 150 percent, with performances taking place five to seven days a week, four times a day. In 2002, the foundation funded the company with another $600,000 grant. As of 2004, the company consists of an artistic director, an executive producer, an associate producer/dramaturge, and approximately thirty-five contract artists per year. In addition to approximately 275 live theatre performances each year, the company offers 150 to 175 storytelling sessions annually.

The Frederick R. Weisman Museum of Art was established in 1934, when it was known as the Little Gallery. Several decades later it became the University of Minnesota Art Museum. In 1993 it was renamed after its major donor and experienced a complete rebirth with a move to a new building, designed by Frank Gehry. "We knew," says Colleen Sheehy, director of education, "that we wanted innovative programs that would make the most of new theories of museum education. We knew that we wanted to engage students and faculty from a wide range of departments, not just those in art and art history. We also wanted to serve as an amiable meeting place between the University of Minnesota and the Twin Cities community. Our experiences with using performance as part of our education programs began in late 1993 when we opened our new museum building." The Weisman uses "an experimental, nonlinear approach to theatre rather than realistic portrayals." It presents commissioned plays, dramatic readings, storytelling, spoken word events, performance art, dance, and music programs, envisioned and planned as part of the museum's educational events. Sometimes theatre pieces use the same style as the visual art they are interpreting. The Weisman uses live performances as a means of "providing insight into a topic or issue or aesthetic, allowing us to connect and support the careers of writers, directors, actors, dancers, and other theatre artists. As an art museum, that is another important role that we play in the community." There is rarely a charge for these performances, which take place in exhibit areas and in the museum's 120-seat auditorium, the Shepherd Room.

The Wheaton History Center is an Illinois museum and education center housed in a 2,200-square-foot, Queen Anne–style, 1887 structure. The center's eight full-time staff members feel that in order to appreciate history, students need to feel and touch it, and that theatre in its broadest sense makes this happen. The center serves learning disabled, behavioral disability, English as a second language, and alternative schools. Programs incorporate first-person and costumed third-person interpretation and presentations; some education programs also incorporate role-playing. The main gallery, the Kiebler, can be transformed into the interior of a slave cabin, and the basement houses a re-created Underground Railroad station.

The Whitaker Center for Science and the Arts opened in Harrisburg, Pennsylvania, in September 1999. It is made up of three parts: the Sunoco Performance Theatre, the Select Medical IMAX, and the Harsco Science Center, as well as a black box theatre. As the Whitaker Center grew, a special space, the Big Science Theatre, was created for performances. "This space," says George Buss, theatre and outreach manager, "has forty-eight dimmers and as many lights, a sound system and tech booth. We also take our shows onto the exhibit floor with highly portable presentations. On the lowest level of the Science Center is our Kids Hall, dedicated to the younger guests." Whitaker on Wheels, the museum's outreach program, goes to schools, malls, libraries, and fairs. The performance program began with "lighthearted, character-based demonstrations" exploring the worlds of electricity, chemistry, physics, entomology, and numerous other scientific areas.

The Witte Museum was founded in 1926 with a natural history collection. The museum is located on the edge of the 450-acre Brackenridge Park. The museum grounds, four and a half acres on the banks of the San Antonio River, include a courtyard garden and received an "Urban Habitat" designation from the National Wildlife Federation. The Bank of America Gallery Theater presents live performances of original history, science, and culture plays daily. Witte performers have also appeared at elementary, middle, high school, and college campuses, and at other area museums, hotel convention facilities, church activity centers, and corporate facilities.

By the time this book reaches your hands it is entirely possible that some of the programs referred to here will have diminished, grown, or—sadly—ceased to be. Their closing would not reflect on their quality. Interpretive programs are often low on an institution's financial totem pole, and museum theatre programs are among the first to go. Whether they are fixed stars in the firmament of museum theatre or fleeting ones, it has been my privilege to honor and record their contributions.

What Is Museum Theatre?

Jan: Do you blame Dad for the choices you've made?

Nate: What choices? Do you call living under a death sentence a choice? Do I wish the test had been available when Dad was young? Yes! Do I wish he'd never had kids? Yes! This is no way to live!

Jan and Nate are siblings whose father has been diagnosed with Huntington's disease, an inherited, crippling, and deadly malady. By focusing on the emotional consequences of confirming whether or not they have the gene for the disease, Jan and Nate take the museum theatre audience on an intense and informative journey into the pros and cons of genetic testing.

Not all museum theatre performances are this dramatic. Many are humorous, fanciful, and lighthearted. There are, in fact, so many styles of museum theatre, encompassing such a wide array of subjects, that the term itself has come into question. Do the words *museum theatre* cover *any* kind of interpretation utilizing theatrical techniques?

The label has been used to describe the following:

- Performances of scripted pieces by actors in defined spaces
- Performances of improvised (unscripted) pieces by actors in defined spaces
- Roving, costumed characters engaging audiences in unscripted dialogue presented by paid, unpaid, professional, and amateur performers

- Living history—costumed characters who may or may not have theatrical training, engaging audiences in unscripted dialogue
- Reenactments—costumed characters who may or may not have theatrical training, carrying out a planned activity
- Performances by youth, designed to integrate them into the museum (not necessarily connected to the subject matter of the institution's exhibits or collections)
- Demonstrations utilizing theatrical techniques, such as special effects or costuming
- Educational activities presented by actors
- Mascots—typically animals or fanciful creations, interacting with children

However, as Gigi Dornfest, director of the Science Discovery Theatre for the Lawrence Hall of Science, puts it, "Disparate theatrical techniques do not, by themselves, create a work of theatre." For Dornfest, "the definitive test" determining where the difference lies between a piece of museum theatre and presentations or demonstrations is: "First, does the piece evoke a different time and place? That is to say, is the imagination of the audience engaged to the point that their world expands to include the story that is before them? In such a situation, the script and the abilities of the actors become the agents of emotional transport. The second element needed to differentiate demos from theatre is the narrative structure. Theatre tells a story."

According to *Webster's*, a theatre is a "building for dramatic performances," or "dramatic representation as an art or profession," but museum theatre may or may not include "a building for dramatic performances," and its "dramatic representations" may or may not be considered the "art or profession" of those presenting them. Points of view regarding what constitutes museum theatre vary greatly. Lucía Todone, innovator of the museum theatre technique in Latin America, believes that the term simply encompasses all available theatrical techniques placed at the museum's service. Commercial theatre, she says, has an end in and of itself, whereas museum theatre is linked indissolubly to a museum's values, its objectives, and its public. Mellissa Marlowe, gallery theatre performer and coordinator for the Witte Museum, adds that "museum theatre suggests plays written specifically to complement museum exhibits or museum educational activities."

Lee Oestreicher, former director of educational programming at the Baltimore Maritime Museum, writes of theatre that its "deepest roots are in the stuff of spirit and imagination, in myth, story, and ritual, in celebration and fantasy. In other words, theater operates in a realm that our culture patronizingly calls 'fiction,' an odd term to apply to those things that make us most truly human." He goes on to say,

> Museum theater, by a strange twist of fate, seems to have become the last form of truly popular theater, the last theater intended for a "nontheatrical" audience. Museum plays tend to be seen by whoever happens to be there, and even pre-booked audiences are museum visitors first and theater-goers next. Museum theater pieces are created for museum visitors—in all of their diversity—and not for that highly self-selected, dedicated audience that supports the regular theater.[1]

This is an important insight, emphasizing that the intended audience plays an important part in defining museum theatre. Our audiences typically have not made a choice to come to our museums to see a play, they have made no financial commitment to the experience by paying for a ticket, and they feel free to come and go throughout the performance.

Museum theatre is frequently the only theatre our audiences see, and it is all the more vital and important for that reason. At the end of a performance an actor could just as readily be asked a question regarding the scientific or historical content of a piece he performed as he could be asked to explain his costume or hairstyle. The answers he provides have equal educational value.

Patricia Decker of Explora believes that while "museum theatre and commercial theatre programs are similar, it is the venue or place that differs. . . . In commercial theatre, the performance place *is* the theatre." Paul Taylor, formerly of the Philadelphia Zoo Treehouse, tells us that "the sole distinction that designates a piece as museum theatre begins in its roots. While theatre can be enlightening, it is not generally bound to the idea that it must teach something. In museum theatre, the genesis usually has contained within its seed the understanding that the piece will relay some educational idea to the audience." In trying to define museum theatre, Taylor and his colleagues in the zoo and aquarium community concluded that an act of theatre was taking place when a character or characters presented a story or a conflict. Character, Taylor believes, is a key element of the transformation theatre aims for—transformation of space, mood, or point of view. According to this definition many types of presentations could be considered theatre, with the exception, Taylor cautions, of "full-bodied mascots" who "often cannot speak and therefore do not have a story to tell." He suggests that "the vast majority of what is labeled museum theatre are presentations that use theatrical techniques." These techniques can include lighting, sets, costumes, sound effects, music, storytelling, puppetry, role-playing and creative dramatics, circus skills (such as juggling and stilt walking), and mask work.

George Buss, of the Whitaker Center for Science and the Arts, believes that "museum theatre exists to make the visitor care enough to learn." Buss has a novel way of characterizing museum theatre, breaking it down into three categories:

- "Demonstration museum theatre, relying on the convention of a demonstration or experiment to draw the audience's attention and create an interest in the science or topic surrounding it"
- "Character-based museum theatre, introducing the audience to a person, fictional or not, so that they can evoke an emotion about the person they are portraying"
- "Plot-based museum theatre, relying on the conventions of the plot to create intrigue and interest"

All three styles have the same goal: "to evoke emotion for the purpose of learning." Buss maintains that "the only negative reaction to a theatre experience is apathy."

Larry Gard of the Science Museum of Virginia says, "A museum educator might answer the question 'What is museum theatre?' by pointing out that a commercial theatre production focuses on entertainment as its ultimate goal. A commercial theatre producer might point out that educational theatre focuses on teaching a lesson as its ultimate goal. I believe that 'museum theatre' is a category of 'educational theatre.'" Gard maintains that "in order for educational theatre to be successful, it must, first and foremost, be good theatre. When I direct a 'museum theatre' production, I reach for the same artistic goals and have the same artistic expectations that I would if I were directing a 'commercial theatre' production." Both Gard and Taylor use the words *engaging, accurate, colorful, vibrant, active, compelling, passionate,* and *inviting* to describe museum theatre.

The National Museum of Science and Industry in London describes the various styles of performance they utilize in this way:

- Naturalistic/environmental—exhibits "inhabited by characters"—a form of living history
- Demonstration—"a demonstration of a scientific or technological principle . . . utilizing a variety of theatrical styles ranging from strong narrative to music hall/burlesque"
- Conversational interaction—"used where large group presentations are inappropriate . . . often involves a tour"
- Public forum/meeting—"the character invites people to debate a principle or development"
- Role-play encouraging active participation—"children are encouraged to play an active 'real' role and information is imparted via conversation"
- Strong narrative presentation—"the telling of a story"
- Public relations/roll-up presentation—"a very open and brash style ideally suited to busy areas"

I believe that *what* is presented, *where*, *by*, and *for whom* define museum theatre, and that this definition matters to the institution utilizing theatre, to theatre practitioners, to audiences, and, ultimately, to program funders. Defining our terms and using them judiciously can only be of benefit to everyone involved. As institutions, we need to be clear about the type of programming we choose to present. Audiences appreciate knowing what to expect from a presentation: if we promote a demonstration as a theatre performance, disappointment or confusion can follow. Applicants for jobs also benefit from clarity. Inviting actors to audition for a *museum theatre* program that does not include what most actors define as acting (assuming a character and performing in a play) will not promote good relations with the theatrical community. Many funders are well aware of the differences between museum theatre performances and demonstrations that utilize theatrical techniques.

Museum theatre begins with *content-based educational performances*, typically shorter than those in theatre venues and frequently interactive, performed *in formal and informal theatre spaces*, both within the museum and as outreach, *by trained museum theatre professionals for museum audiences of all ages* and for school audiences.

Museum theatre, then, contains the following elements:

- Its purpose is educational and linked to the institution's mission and values.
- It aims for high artistic quality by employing trained professionals, paid and unpaid.
- Performances are typically shorter than those in theatre venues, and frequently interactive.

Many people believe that museum theatre provides another tool for conveying information, but Michael List of the Carnegie Museum of Natural History reminds us that "good theatre should never become a series of instructions." It "is not just a scientific lecture that borrows some theatrical techniques." In fact, as I regularly remind participants in the annual Theatre in Museums Workshop, as a conveyor of information, theatre is not at its best. Theatre is a catalyst, a motivator, a means of encouraging audiences to want to encounter and wrestle with ideas. Theatre fosters an imaginative, creative, and culturally diverse understanding of the objects we choose to display—and sometimes of those we don't choose to display. It achieves this by adding the personal—a sense of time, a sense of space, and a story.

WHAT THEATRE CAN DO

A decade ago, the American Association of Museums published *Excellence and Equity: Education and the Public Dimension of Museums*. In this report, readers are asked to consider: "How can museums—as multidimensional, socially responsible institutions with a tremendous capacity for bringing knowledge to the public and enriching all facets of the human experience—help to nurture a humane citizenry equipped to make informed choices in a democracy and to address the challenges and opportunities of an increasingly global society?" These ideas—that museums are socially responsible, that our humanity may need nurturing, and that making informed choices in a democracy is an important function—are not always at the forefront of conversations devoted to exhibit development and program planning. In an era when citizens' greatest value to society can easily be reduced to our function as "consumers," museum offerings are often just another item on the consumption menu.

This can be galling to those of us who are drawn to work in museums precisely because they nurture our humanity. When I ask museum colleagues what they most value about their work, they often answer that working in a museum is like being paid to further one's education. "Every day something new comes in the door!" one said. "My curiosity is always being fed," another added. Some emphasize the highly creative atmosphere that pervades museums, creativity that encompasses the visual (as in exhibit design), crowd management techniques, advertising, writing labels and teacher materials, and, of course, performances.

Disengagement and disenchantment creep in when mixed messages are perceived, when a museum's choices regarding exhibits and expenditures appear to contradict its larger, more "socially responsible" mission. At this point, theatre can often come to a museum's aid. Theatre thrives on conflict and inquiry and is invaluable in inspiring people, challenging them, and making them less fearful of encountering ideas, especially those foreign or new to them. Theatrical characters can embody what we most love and most fear; couched in a theatrical performance, issues can be discussed and examined in a nonthreatening way, and we can be invited to laugh and to cry about ourselves and others.

Theatre can occasionally even be used to examine the internal workings of museums themselves, and the contradictory messages often conveyed by official and unofficial policies, as in the play *The Object of Their Affections*, commissioned in 1989 by the Western Museums Conference and written by Lee Oestreicher. The object in the title is a hat rack—not any hat rack, but a hat rack donated by one of the museum's most influential donors. An inquiry from the president of the institution as to where this hat rack may have been stored generates a flurry of activity, from a search to the inclusion of the hat rack in an exhibit on the development of Western civilization. During the course of being found and displayed, the hat rack passes through the hands of conservators, educators, designers, and fund-raisers, all of whom are satirized with equal affection by the playwright for their individual and collective eccentricities. This play is lighthearted and uses humor as the means for examining human behavior, but people in extreme situations also often credit playfulness and imagination with saving their lives and their sanity. Both play and the use of the imagination are the stuff of theatre. Play allows us to use our imaginations to transform reality, spaces, moods, and even points of view.

In her master's thesis, "Museum Theatre: Its History and Practice," Edith Serkownek examines the transformative power of historical pageants, which "were believed to be instruments of positive *community transformation* by showing a patriotic, unified, and empowering version of the past and involving the whole community in its creation." She goes on to say that pageantry "generally accomplished this task by evoking the history of a community through a series of episodes showing its members working, playing and overcoming numerous common obstacles. The pageant often ended with a view of the community's bright future based on the lessons learned from the past."[2]

Dornfest believes that "theatre can *transform* nearly any *space* into a performance arena. Whether it is the museum floor, a school cafeteria or a county fair." One of the most extraordinary space transformations I have seen took place at the Museo de Historia Natural in Montevideo, Uruguay. The museum consists of three floors of natural history collections, displayed in glass cases. Through the center of the building there is an open stairwell, with wrought-iron railings from which one can look down to the floors below. Due to the absence of natural light, the stairwell and the ground floor can be effectively lit by stage lighting. For its play *A la deriva* ("Adrift"), museum theatre producers hung sacking from one level to another, the rough fabric giving the impression of deep river banks. The level from which the play could be viewed was dimly lit, and the audience looked down the river banks at the floor below, where a canoe was turning. The play is set in a wooded area, and with the use of theatrical lighting, animals and birds in the surrounding display cases had been carefully selected and lit so ably that the display cases themselves were invisible.

Marlowe of the Witte believes that museum theatre can *transform points of view* by "tackling . . . 'hidden' history, history that is rarely taught in schools and is not often discussed." She gives as an example *Noble Lofton, Buffalo Soldier*, a play examining the life of black soldiers in the U.S. Army in the late nineteenth century. Sheehy of the Weisman agrees. Her museum presented a gallery performance piece to accompany their Jacob Lawrence exhibition, and Sheehy writes of the performance that it "definitely prompted a change in *mood* and *point of view*, encouraging people to feel, from the inside, what such historical figures as Harriet Tubman, Toussaint L'Ouverture, and John Brown felt and experienced and why they held such strong convictions that they would risk—and give—their lives for the cause of freedom" (emphasis mine).

Theatre, then, is a transformational art, capable of teaching through the emotions, of inspiring hope and positive change, and therefore of being a force to improve our world. Can one ask for more?

Museums, George E. Hein and Mary Alexander tell us, "make content and ideas accessible, facilitating intellectual connections and bringing together disparate facts, ideas and feelings. Museums affect values and attitudes, for example, facilitating comfort with cultural differences or developing environmental ethics. Museums promote cultural, community and familial identity. Museums foster visitor interest and curiosity, inspiring self-confidence and motivation to pursue future learning and life choices. Museums affect *how* visitors think and approach their worlds, in contrast to *what* they think."[3] As one actor put it after reading this description, the marriage between museums and theatre seems made in heaven.

These are some very basic differences and similarities between traditional and museum theatre.

Differences

In most *traditional theatres* we pay an admission fee and take our seats within clearly defined spaces—one space for the audience, another for the performers.

Many *museum theatre* experiences are free of charge (or included in the admission fee) and may take place within exhibition spaces, with no, or very limited, seating provided for audiences.

The subject matter of the play bears no relationship to the premises in which the play is performed.

The subject matter is related to the museum as a whole or to the exhibit within which the performance takes place.

Performances typically last at least ninety minutes.

Performances rarely last longer than half an hour.

Performers only occasionally acknowledge the audience or interact with them during or the after the show.

Performers usually acknowledge the audience and frequently interact with them both during and after performance.

That Ol' Windbag, *performed by Larry Gard. Photograph reprinted with permission of the Science Museum of Virginia.*

Similarities

Performances may include props, costumes, sets, lighting, and sound. There are actors involved, speaking previously agreed-on lines. The performance has been directed and technically supported.

NOTES

1. Oestreicher, "Museum Theater: Coming of Age," *Journal of Museum Education* 15 (Spring/Summer 1990), 4–15.

2. Serkownek, "Museum Theatre: Its History and Practice" (master's thesis, Cooperstown Graduate Program, State University of New York, Oneonta, 1998) (emphasis mine).

3. Hein and Alexander, *Museums: Places of Learning*, American Association of Museums Education Committee Professional Practice Series (Washington, DC: American Association of Museums, 1998).

2

A Brief History

While researching the life of Elizabeth Blackwell (the first woman in the United States to receive an accredited medical degree, in 1849), I came across some intriguing words she wrote after visiting the American Museum of Natural History in New York City: "saw a wretched piece of acting and some horrid mock mummies." Could it be, I wondered, that museum theatre is actually over a century old? If so, what a pity that its first review should be so dismal! Regrettably, no amount of digging unearthed any information about what the "wretched piece of acting" was, until I read Edith Serkownek's thesis and saw the words, "Showmen such as Phineas Taylor Barnum, the creator of several successful museums in mid-nineteenth century America, flourished by giving the public exhibits, 'curiosities,' and theatrical entertainment." Barnum's American Museum in New York "featured a Moral Lecture Room where moral plays and farces were presented, sometimes as many as twelve in one day."[1] Indeed, author Charles Coleman Sellers asserts that "Barnum claimed credit for being the first to transform the museum lecture room into a playhouse in all but name."[2] If there was some error in Blackwell's recording of where she viewed the "wretched piece of acting," this would explain her disappointment. Perhaps what she saw was one of these farces at Barnum's American Museum, not the American Museum of Natural History.

Traditional museums, Serkownek goes on to say, "distanced themselves from such 'popular' theatrical activities," but nevertheless during the nineteenth century museums began developing dioramas to display their biological collections, borrowing heavily from the art of the theatrical set designer. Serkownek cites Stephen Eddy Snow, who writes of nineteenth-century theatre and museums: "In what might be characterized as a reciprocity of means and complementarity of function, museums used the theatrical craft of scene painting for exhibits and staged performances in their lecture rooms, while theatre used the subjects presented in museums."[3]

Along with the development of dioramas and sets for the display of natural history, props and costumes also began to be used in historical sites. Swedish educator Arthur Hazelius introduced Americans to the use of *tableaux vivants*—described by Serkownek as "human habitat groupings which featured mannequins posed in domestic scenes." Hazelius believed that artifacts could not really be understood when removed from their context, which led him in 1881 to create reproductions of houses, schools, and farms at a living history site called Skansen in his native Sweden. Seven years later, Hazelius added performers and costumed guides to recreate historic settings; following his example, in 1909 costumed guides appeared at the John Ward House in Salem, Massachusetts. Colonial Williamsburg followed suit in 1932, including costumed craft demonstrators at its site. "Open-air museums," Serkownek says, "had, in effect, become performance spaces—and at the same time exhibits in many traditional museums were transformed into theater sets, complete with painted scenery."[4] The courtship between museums and the theatre was in full swing!

By the mid-1950s, the National Park Service had been instrumental in developing open-air museums with live interpretation. Typically, as stated in the Forest History Center's staff manual, the stories told at these sites were "of the best, cleanest and happiest memories of America. No dirt, manure, poor or social problems were allowed to emerge to tarnish the nostalgic image of the past."[5]

It was one of the Park Service's own employees, Freeman Tilden, who questioned this approach, which in turn led to reenactments of battles and similar recreations of historical pageantry. Frequently, these reenactments were of Revolutionary and Civil War battles, often held on the original battlefields. Organizers were sticklers for accuracy and firm believers in historical reenactments as a means toward establishing community involvement, and in collaborations between academics and local talent of all sorts—performers, costumers, and local historians.

The 1960s brought enormous societal changes, with revolutionary approaches to gender and race issues. Women, African Americans, Asian Americans, and Hispanic Americans influenced the way history was taught, including the points of view of those whom history had typically ignored and discounted: women, children, slaves, and the poor and disenfranchised. These stories were often personal in nature, emotional, and dramatic. History centers and historical sites were not slow to appreciate this rich source of information, and to recognize a sure way of engaging large numbers of visitors by helping them relate history to their own daily lives, giving dignity and importance to household and farm chores, and presenting the points of view of the common man, woman, and child.

The Forest History Center credits the Association for Living History Farms and Agricultural Museums, founded in 1970, with leading the way in building "better mission statements" and in using information to relate to the visitor's experience and reveal the life behind the artifact or setting. They also advocated presenting information "with imagination" and in ways "that will provoke the visitor into thinking for himself rather than simply being instructed, and information that will provide a larger picture of the artifact or setting,"[6] a philosophy based on Tilden's principles. In the early 1950s, as a result of his work for the National Park Service defining the foundational principles of interpretation, Tilden wrote a book called *Interpreting Our Heritage*. His book is considered a classic work that forever changed our approach to interpretation. Tilden's seven principles are as follows:

- Any interpretation that does not somehow relate what is being displayed or described to something within the personality or experience of the visitor will be sterile.
- Interpretation addressed to children should not be a dilution of the presentation to adults, but should follow a fundamentally different approach. To be at its best it will require a separate program.
- Information, as such, is not interpretation. Interpretation is revelation based on information. But they are entirely different things.
- Interpretation is an educational activity that aims to reveal meanings and relationships rather than simply to communicate factual information.

- The chief aim of interpretation is not instruction but provocation.
- Interpretation is an art that combines many arts, whether the materials presented are scientific, historic, or architectural. Any art is in some degree teachable.
- Interpretation should aim to present a whole, rather than a part, and must address itself to the whole man rather than any phase.

In 1969, the American Association of Museums published *America's Museums: The Belmont Report*, documenting "the incredible growth in museum use over the previous thirty years, the expansion of programs and services, new methods of interpretation, and the changing roles of many museums." The report also raised questions regarding a museum's audiences and their expectations of a museum visit. It stated that

> American museums were . . . established to collect, preserve, exhibit and interpret objects of art or history or science. These remain their basic functions. Never-the-less, many museums now serve as concert halls or theaters or meeting-places for various organized groups. Nearly all large art museums, and apparently more than half of the smaller ones, sponsor or offer their facilities for musical programs, drama, ballet and dance performances.[7]

This trend, Serkownek points out, "came to be incorporated into the architecture of the museum. Museums built during this era generally included not only galleries, offices, and storage space, but also spaces such as auditoriums, club rooms, and meeting rooms."[8]

In their 1975 study *Museum Sponsorship of the Performing Arts*, Cynthia K. Madle and Robert M. Kerr state that, of the 124 museums that responded to their questionnaire, 41 sponsored drama, 9 mime, and 5 puppet shows.[9] "However," Serkownek points out, "from the data provided it is difficult to determine how many of the museums surveyed . . . were presenting museum theatre."[10] Another unknown is whether any of the performances supported the museums' goals or whether they were created specifically to meet those goals.

During the second half of the twentieth century, museums were moving away from static, hands-off exhibits and toward interactive, hands-on activities. Nowhere was this more evident than in children's museums. In *Doing*

Children's Museums: A Guide to 225 Hands-On Museums, Joanne Cleaver credits the Boston Children's Museum with pioneering the hands-on approach. Science museums were not far behind. There, "exhibits were not viewed, but performed," Serkownek says, "either by the visitor or by staff members trained as demonstrators."[11]

Apart from first-person interpretation and historical reenactments, one of the first productions that can be classified as museum theatre took place at Old Sturbridge Village in 1961. It was called *The Pangs of Liberty* and was written by a commissioned playwright and performed by professional actors.

A decade later, three museums began experimenting with the use of theatre in their galleries. One was the Smithsonian's National Portrait Gallery. In 1972 the gallery developed *The Trial of John Brown*, which included a long reenactment of John Brown's trial for treason in 1859.[12] As described by Lee Oestreicher,

> museum staff performed the piece before a jury of students, usually in a high school setting. Later, the same students visited the Portrait Gallery and participated in a role-playing activity, adopting the identities of archetypal characters from the era of John Brown, e.g., slaves, free blacks, slave owners, and abolitionists. A tour of the museum's collections relating to this period in American history followed this activity.[13]

Another of these pioneers was the Science Museum of Minnesota, which started incorporating theatre into its exhibits in a formal way when a young woman called Sondra Quinn approached Phillip Taylor, the museum's director, with a proposal for blending her love of teaching, theatre, and museums. Taylor, a farsighted and creative man, was drawn to Quinn's ideas but lacked the funds with which to establish a theatre program. He put his creativity to work and found a modest amount of money unallocated in the museum's security budget. He asked Quinn if she would be willing to come to work for the museum as a security guard—specifically to guard the moon rock then on display—and on the side develop an experimental museum theatre program. Quinn accepted and was soon working on a puppet show for the Anthropology Hall featuring two anthropologists called Pete and Doc. (They have earned their place in museum history and now reside in SMM's collections vault.)

Pete and Doc were extremely popular, and Taylor and Quinn, encouraged, moved on to produce character cameos, one-person monologues examining not only the scientific contributions of the characters portrayed, but their feelings about their discoveries, frustrations, family issues, and personal conflicts. As the program grew, Quinn hired writing interns to develop the scripts, little knowing that among the aspiring playwrights developing scripts for her was a future Pulitzer Prize winner—August Wilson.

As a result of various presentations Quinn made in the 1970s at American Association of Museums and Association of Science Technology Centers conferences, other institutions gradually became interested in her interpretive techniques and her educational findings. Quinn was busy writing articles about museum theatre and breaking new ground with her program when a series of budget cuts rendered the program inoperative, and for two years it ceased to exist. Interestingly, the program was cut because it was considered one of the easiest to re-fund, which proved to be true. By the time funds were in place to reinstate the program two years later, Quinn was preparing to assume a vice presidency. It was then that she hired a full-time theatre programs coordinator to pick up where she had left off and to organize the first Theatre in Museums Workshop, which took place in 1984. Quinn had perceived sufficient interest in the museum community to offer a three-day workshop focusing exclusively on the use of theatre. It was attended by representatives from twelve museums and set the stage for the eighteen workshops that have followed. The Theatre in Museums Workshop now runs for six days and is divided into two parts. Part I focuses on the basics of establishing and running a museum theatre program, and Part II is devoted to the development of scripts.

The third pioneer was the Museum of Science and Industry in Chicago, where, as reported by Serkownek,

> between 1972 and 1973, the museum presented Science Playhouse, a series of four plays exploring different aspects of science and the lives of scientists. The plays were performed by a professional group associated with the Art Institute of Chicago. These productions included both borrowed scripts and original plays created specifically for the museum. . . . A 1979 survey revealed that in a two and a half year period, thirty different plays were presented at the institution with an average attendance of 600 people per performance.[14]

In *A Stage for Science*, the Association of Science-Technology Centers (ASTC), reports that "nearly all ASTC museums offer a variety of demonstration and dramatic programs on a regular basis. In the period 1977–1979, some 22 million people of all ages saw over 2,000 different performances at ASTC museums."

The 1990s saw the emergence of two organizations dedicated to furthering museum theatre, the International Museum Theatre Alliance, or IMTAL, founded by Catherine Hughes of the Boston Museum of Science, and the Museum Theatre Professional Interest Council, under the auspices of the American Association of Museums. Surveys conducted by both groups estimate that in the United States over one hundred museums, zoos, aquariums, and historic sites now use museum theatre regularly. Only a handful house a resident, full-time theatre team, but many employ professional actors seasonally or for special events, and several run outreach theatre programs.

NOTES

1. Serkownek, "Museum Theatre."

2. Sellers, *Mr. Peale's Museum: Charles Peale and the First Popular Museum of Natural Science and Art* (New York: Norton, 1980), 1–14.

3. Snow, *Performing the Pilgrims: A Study of Ethnohistorical Role-Playing at Plimoth Plantation* (Jackson: University Press of Mississippi, 1993), quoted in Serkownek, "Museum Theatre."

4. Serkownek, "Museum Theatre."

5. Forest History Center's Staff Manual.

6. As quoted by Serkownek in "Museum Theatre."

7. American Association of Museums, *American Museums: The Belmont Report* (Washington, DC: American Association of Museums, 1969).

8. Serkownek, "Museum Theatre."

9. Cynthia K. Mandel and Robert M. Kerr, *Museum Sponsorship of Performing Arts* (Center for Arts Administration, Graduate School of Business, University of Wisconsin, Madison, 1975), quoted in Serkownek, "Museum Theatre."

10. Serkownek, "Museum Theatre."

11. Serkownek, "Museum Theatre."

12. The use of educational theatre techniques at the Portrait Gallery was pioneered by Dennis O'Toole, its first curator of education.

13. Oestreicher, "Museum Theatre: The Beginnings of a Natural Alliance," *Museum Theatre Journal* (September 1993).

14. Serkownek, "Museum Theatre."

3

The Interpretive Palette

Few museum theatre practitioners are in a position to hire a large number of performers. Some don't have a stage to perform on, and some have to do all of the development and production work with few of the resources available to a theatre, such as technical support and a stock of props and costumes. Even with these limitations, it is still possible to draw from a rich array of theatrical techniques and styles to create a vibrant theatre program. What follows is just a sampler, not an exhaustive list of styles. These categories represent various techniques successfully employed in museums. Needless to say, the various elements can be mixed and matched—a monologue can include puppets, storytelling can be interactive, and so on.

STORYTELLING

Telling stories is very probably where it all began, sitting around a cave fire, perhaps, during long winter nights. Storytelling as an art form has traditions, a history, and a literature all its own. Organized groups of storytellers attend conventions and meetings, and often make their living by telling stories to people of all ages. Sometimes, storytellers focus on a subject or theme. Always, they have their own style of performing.

The Metropolitan Museum of Art began using storytelling in 1917 with Anna Curtis Chandler, who worked in the photography department of the Metropolitan's library. Curtis Chandler was interested in expanding the museum's education program by writing and adapting art-related stories, illustrated with lantern slides. Dr. Barbara Fleisher Zucker describes these programs:

> She would . . . guide children into the galleries to see collections related to her story, or in the case of the large Sunday audience, told visitors where they could find the works of art. Her story themes were not just about paintings, but artists and artisans, their work, and the times in which they lived. . . . The storyteller, she declared, must throw herself into the different parts of the story, make the characters live for the audience, and become so familiar with her characters that there will be no hunting for words.[1]

Anna Curtis Chandler went on to tell stories at the Cleveland Museum of Art, the Museum of Fine Art (Boston), and the Worcester Art Museum. She also published several volumes of museum stories. She conducted after-school programs in which "children posed as works of art, created tableaux, and presented original plays . . . in connection with the museum's collections."[2] Later in her storytelling career she performed at the Kaufmann Auditorium on 92nd Street, relating her programs to various museums all over New York City.

Museums have employed storytellers to tell children's tales, to appear in costume and weave stories around particular exhibits, and for cultural purposes—to share traditions, history, myths, and folk stories. Explora Science Center and Children's Museum for example, offers a storytelling experience for Chinese New Year. The Pacific Science Center in Seattle uses storytelling along with song and dance to teach audiences about Native American culture and heritage.[3]

Storytelling as museum theatre may involve an actor not necessarily described as a storyteller. In *The Road From Ban Vinai*, an actor appears in the Hmong House at the Science Museum of Minnesota, portraying a former U.S. Air Force pilot, and invites people to gather round and listen to him tell stories about his experiences with the Hmong during the Vietnam War.

MONOLOGUES

The actor delivering a monologue may be portraying a real or imagined character from any time period, or may even portray more than one character during the course of the performance. If your museum can hire more than one actor and produce more than one show, monologues offer the ultimate in versatility. Rather than commit the entire performance group to one time and place, casting two actors in two different monologues gives a museum four different shows to draw from.

HISTORICAL CHARACTERS

Historical characters represent real, once living people, brought to life through the power of theatre to share their lives, work, and times with an audience. Performers may address the audience and engage in brief interactions with them. The performers wear historically accurate period costume, and may have set items reflecting the period. Examples of historical figures that have been presented this way are George Washington Carver, Marie Curie, Charles Darwin, Frederick Douglass, Galileo Galilei, Thomas Jefferson, Margaret Mead, and Nikola Tesla.

PARTICIPATORY AND INTERACTIVE THEATRE

Participatory implies that members of the audience are invited to join the performer for an activity or exercise. *Interactive* implies that audience members are acknowledged as being present and may engage in dialogue with the performer, without leaving their seats. Participatory theatre includes pieces on the history and significance of folk dancing and games around the world. During the performance of these pieces, audience members are taught a dance or a game and actually dance or play with the performers. Interactive theatre might take the form of a puppet show about the color spectrum during which children, without leaving their seats, are asked to identify colors or engage in dialogue with the puppeteer.

It is important to keep in mind that both performers and audiences typically need to be helped to feel comfortable with participatory and interactive theatre. One of the best performers I ever trained in museum theatre had never performed interactively before and it took her over a year to feel at ease inviting audience participation. Other performers take readily to this technique. Audiences frequently need to be encouraged to participate—by performers who are nonthreatening (do not coerce participation), respectful (do not make fun of anyone who volunteers, except with their previous consent), and appreciative of the

Albert Einstein, *performed by Eric Meyer. Photograph reprinted with permission of the Explora Science Center and Children's Museum.*

George Washington Carver, *performed by Don Perkins. Photograph reprinted with permission of the Explora Science Center and Children's Museum.*

participation. It is not difficult to engage an audience if these guidelines are observed. The temptation to bring a volunteer up on stage and make fun of him or her is overwhelming to some performers and needs to be resisted. It is as easy and just as funny to make the presenter the butt of the jokes. An example of an exception to this rule is *Clowning around with Physics*, a clown act created by Stephanie Long at SMM to accompany the traveling exhibit Science under the Big Top, developed by the Ontario Science Center. Here a member of the audience was asked before the show whether he would be willing to don a tutu and join the two clowns during their act. Many willing and prepared volunteers then took the plunge, some of them outdoing the clowns in their efforts to entertain and clearly enjoying the opportunity to, literally, clown around.

Another important guideline to keep in mind when interacting with an audience is that, just as in sales, the customer is always right. No matter what an audience member answers, the performer responds positively. This does not mean that incorrect answers to factual questions are passed off as correct, but that the presenter affirms the person for participating by saying, "Good guess!" or "You're close!"

Last but not least, I discourage presenters from applauding participants, for a very simple reason—they may remember to applaud some and not others. Equal appreciation for everyone courageous enough to participate in the show helps guarantee that audiences will trust the presenter and be glad they took part.

PLAYS ADDRESSING CONTROVERSIAL
OR OTHERWISE CHALLENGING SUBJECTS

Here is where theatre often comes into its own. Examples of topics examined by museums through the use of theatre are racial, age, gender, and religious discrimination; medical ethics, including organ transplants and other life-and-death concerns; population; and a vast array of ecological and environmental topics. Facts that a museum would be loath to print on labels, or questions it would hesitate to raise in other formats, can be addressed in a play. (See chapter 11.)

FOURTH WALL THEATRE

Fourth wall theatre is a traditional form of theatre in which actors on stage do not acknowledge the presence of the audience and perform as if a fourth wall existed between them. I don't recommend this form for open spaces, such as

The Spite Fence *by Patty Lynch, performed by Dawn Reed and Rex Isom, Jr. Photo-graph reprinted with permission of the Minnesota Historical Society.*

galleries. It is difficult for the actors to engage the attention of roving audiences if they are supposed not to know they are there, and the experience of walking by or dropping in on a fourth wall play in a gallery space can be confusing for the audience. It is a viable choice for an enclosed theatre space.

MIME

There are two ways of incorporating mime into a performance. It can be used to demonstrate an action or object within an otherwise nonmimed play, or it can be an entire, silent performance of its own. In either case, it should be done well or not at all. It is an art form in its own right and is best left to those who have studied the form and know how to present it, such as the Seattle Mime Theatre, which performed at the Pacific Science Center and "led audience participation activities in make-up, stretching exercises, and basic facial expressions."[4] The Rochester Museum and Science Center's Strasenburgh Planetarium offered a mime show illustrating the principles of flight.

MUSIC

Instrumental or vocal music can provide a prelude to the show or be an integral part of it. It can be prerecorded or live. Unless one's purpose is to show ineptness or provide humor, live music, like mime, is best left to skilled practitioners.

An example of music as an essential component of a theatre piece is *I Heard an Indian Drum*, a piece that examines the work of Frances Densmore in recording and helping to preserve Native American musical traditions. In it the performer sings excerpts from one or two lullabies and playful songs. Music was at the core of Frances Densmore's research, and the piece focuses on the significance of music to Native American cultural and spiritual life.

The California Museum of Science and Industry developed several musicals, including *A Reason for Seasons*, about natural cycles; *A Case of Missing Matter, or H2O Where Are You?* on liquids, solids, and gases; and *Young Tom Edison*.

At the Lawrence Hall of Science "musical accompaniment is a key element," Dornfest says. "Nothing better sets mood, tempo, or atmosphere. We do not have any programs that are completely without sound effects, music or song."

In San Francisco, the Exploratorium has offered a concert series featuring musicians "in an informal, intimate setting. The musicians perform and answer questions, ranging from how the instrument's shape affects its sound, to the history of the music, and personal values in its interpretation."[5]

DANCE AND MOVEMENT

Movement is a rhythmic, choreographed or improvised activity within a play. It might or might not reflect any particular style or require training to perform. Dance is also rhythmic and may also be choreographed or improvised, but dance moves do reflect a style and do require training to perform well.

The Australian Powerhouse Museum, for example, had actors engaged in the movement of "swimming" through the museum as a way of emphasizing its spaces. The Science Museum of Virginia presented a program spearheaded by the Richmond Ballet, Minds in Motion. Among other activities, it involved children using creative dance to depict the motion of microscopic particles.

Examples of museum theatre performances that consist entirely of choreographed dances are rare. *Praying with Your Feet* at the SMM is one of them; another is *Eddy*, produced by the Weisman and named after the eddying Mississippi River nearby—and the movement of people through the building itself. Sheehy writes that

> when the Weisman first opened, we collaborated with the University of Minnesota's Dance Program with a visiting choreographer, Mel Wong. Wong choreographed a site-specific dance with dance students at the Weisman. His dance, called *Eddy*, moved in a circle through the museum space, where the dancers used the features of the building in unconventional ways, e.g., "walking" up the walls, dancing in the freight elevator, rolling on the floors. Their performance encouraged viewers to think of the space differently and to appreciate its special features.

Praying with Your Feet *by Timothy Cope, performed by Clayton James and Joan Lisi. Photograph reprinted with permission of the Science Museum of Minnesota.*

Normally, Sheehy says, the museum would not encourage performers to walk up its walls, but in this case, she decided that any marks could be easily washed off later. An attitude that emphasizes "the sanctity of the art gallery" prevents innovative uses of the space, Sheehy believes.

PUPPETRY

Puppets come in all shapes and sizes, from finger puppets to elaborate, room-size examples. Michael Judd writes that puppets have a universal appeal and deliver content in a "colorful, entertaining and nonpedantic format."[6] In the spring 1997 edition of the *Journal of Museum Education* (hereafter referred to as the *Journal*), puppeteer Paul Short says,

> What makes a puppet is the puppeteer. . . . A good puppeteer can make almost anything into a puppet—a sock, a sponge, a glove on a hand, a ball, a skein of yarn. This skill or trick, that ability that allows this life to happen, is something which the puppeteer has. . . . A real tree cannot talk, but a puppet tree can. Puppets can confront us on issues with abandon. If we don't like what they say, we have the power to hang them up and no one gets hurt![7]

At the Philadelphia Zoo Treehouse, puppets of various kinds have been used, including rod, life-size, shadow, marionette, sock, and found object puppets. At the SMM, *Indigo Woman* uses one small hand puppet to tell the story of how the color blue came to earth. *Mary's Dinosaur Day*, also at the SMM, a black light (fluorescent) production, includes a sixteen-foot-tall Tyrannosaurus rex and an underwater sequence with schools of prehistoric fish.

At the Lawrence Hall of Science, puppets "have played star roles in several productions," Dornfest says. "Puppets easily create drama and atmosphere, deepening the theatrical experience. They can also provide an illustration of unusual animals that we can't get to actually appear onstage, such as a jellyfish, or as an 'impossible' effect, such as a man reduced to the size of a Barbie doll" (in the play *Tales of the Delta*). Expanding the usefulness of puppets, the Lawrence Hall of Science's Science Discovery Theatre has incorporated soft sculpture costumes and masks. "One actor plays three roles in *Who Let the Smog Out?* S/he puts on a mask and cloak to become Dr. Particulate, and disappears under robes attached to a large, articulated puppet head as the monster Smog itself."

Naomi Stein, director of the Tarnival Street Theatre, who works closely with the Lawrence Hall of Science, describes how,

> in a play about reducing, reusing, recycling, and composting, we reused small, common, household objects as puppets to illustrate the point. These lovable characters included Elvis the Earthworm, Glenda the Glass Bottle and Benny the Bag. They were simple in construction and enlivened by costume—Elvis wore a sequined satin cape and sported a sculpted foam pompadour, while Glenda wore long false eyelashes and a lamé gown. Three life-size puppets were used in *The Wizard of Odds* to portray the Tin Man, the Lion, and the Scarecrow. They "expanded" the cast by allowing one actor to portray these three characters without ever having to leave the stage to change costume.

Trash Bridges: Garbage Detective, *performed by Naomi Stein with Elvis the Earthworm. Photograph reprinted with permission of the Regents of the University of California.*

Mary's Dinosaur Day *by Heidi Arneson. Example of life size puppets. Photograph reprinted with permission of the Science Museum of Minnesota.*

THEATRICAL TOURS

Theatrical tours bear some resemblance to living history, providing occasions on which visitors can meet a variety of characters during the course of a guided tour. An example is the Caesarea on the Sea, King Herod's Dream exhibit at the SMM. During a tour through the exhibit, which displayed various eras of history, the tour guides stopped to introduce people to a Roman harbor builder, a young Byzantine man, and a female Crusader, who appeared briefly to highlight different artifacts in the exhibit and aspects of life in their time.

HOW TO DETERMINE WHICH OF THESE STYLES IS BEST FOR YOU

Before selecting a style, you will need to examine *why* you want to use museum theatre.

Your answer to this question will determine *all* of your choices. However obvious the answer may seem ("We want to increase our attendance," "We believe it to be an effective educational tool," "We need to enliven our museum!"), I encourage you to consider it seriously and to write it down as if you intended to persuade a funder or a board of directors of the merits of your position.

As an illustration, two examples of answers to this question are provided below.

Museum A

We want to use theatre in our museum to draw families with young (under age eight) children to our institution. Theatre will provide us with an opportunity to present colorful, entertaining, and mobile short shows highlighting our exhibits. We are particularly targeting an area of our museum to which younger children are less attracted—our Ecological Imprint of the City exhibit. For the following reasons, this area is an excellent place to prototype our theatre program and the goals we have set for it:

a) It contains a space that can be transformed into a performance space.
b) The exhibits are arranged in such a way that performances can also happen outside the larger performance space.
c) The separate entrance to this area will allow us to test the effects of a small admission fee when performances are taking place.

Museum B

Museum B will soon be moving to new and larger premises. As part of our effort to present a new face to our community, we have rewritten our mission and goals statements to reflect our growing commitment to diversity and to our educational programs. Museum B believes that the use of theatre will meet both these goals by allowing us to hire two actors to develop and perform stories, dances, and plays from a variety of cultures. Performances will have clearly defined educational goals, which could include presenting an important historical figure from the community or sharing a cultural tradition.

What follows is a simple planning chart allowing Museums A and B to make some initial choices regarding location(s) of performances, length of the play, number of actors, budget for props and costumes, and target audience.

MUSEUM A

Location	Length	# of Actors	Budget*	Target Audience
Exhibit	10–15 mins.	3	$2,000	children under 8

*Does not include salaries. Prop and costume expenses only.

Interpretive Palette

	Yes	No	Maybe
Monologues	x		
Controversial topics			x
Fourth wall theatre		x	
Historical monologues		x	
Theatrical tours			x
Participatory/interactive	x		
Storytelling	x		
Mime			x
Music			x
Dance			x
Puppetry	x		

MUSEUM B

Location	Length	# of Actors	Budget*	Target Audience
Exhibits	10–15 mins.	2	$5,000	diverse families
Theatre	15–30 mins.	2	$5,000	diverse families

*Does not include salaries. Prop and costume expenses only.

Interpretive Palette

	Yes	No	Maybe
Monologues	x		
Controversial topics	x		
Fourth wall theatre			x
Historical monologues	x		
Theatrical tours			x
Participatory/interactive	x		
Storytelling	x		
Mime			x
Music	x		
Dance	x		
Puppetry			x

The Good, the Bad, and the Bugly, *performed by George E. Buss and Kasi L. K. Marshall. Photograph reprinted with permission of the Whitaker Center.*

A THEATRE PROGRAM'S PLACE WITHIN THE INSTITUTION

As you determine where to house your theatre program, it is useful to refer yet again to your reasons for doing museum theatre. It may then become obvious that your program belongs in education, member or school services, marketing, or another department. It is also important to consider interactions between museum theatre personnel and other workers.

- Will the exhibits department be building sets or props for your productions?
- Will education or curatorial staff want script approval?
- Will you be performing for schools, and is there staff at your institution already working on school programs?
- Will the theatre program be called on to perform at special museum events?
- Will you be asked to do outreach performances?
- Are volunteers involved with your programs?

In thinking through these connections and relationships, take into account potential conflicts over space, resources, and personnel, and also potential benefits that your institution can derive from the presence of theatre professionals. These benefits are examined in chapter 9 and may include additional public relations and outreach opportunities, and providing staff training in presentation techniques.

Education

Among our sample museums, the following have chosen to place their theatre programs within their education departments:

Explora

The Philadelphia Zoo Treehouse

The Museo de Historia Natural

The Carnegie Museum of Natural History

The Wheaton History Center—one staff member is in charge of education and marketing.

The Frederick R. Weisman Art Museum (the Education Department includes Public Programs and Outreach). In the words of Colleen Sheehy, "As part of the education department, the theatre programs are integrated into our plans for exhibitions and become part of the whole package that we present to funders and then to visitors and audiences."

Exhibits and Programs Department

The Whitaker Center for Science and the Arts has placed its theatre programs within its Exhibits and Programs Department. This department was chosen "to separate public programs from more formal education programs for management purposes. The director of education and the director of exhibits and programs work together to create programming that dovetail together functionally."

Multimedia

At the Carpenter Science Theatre, in the Science Museum of Virginia, the Multimedia Department produces the museum's television and radio programming, and its planetarium shows. "The first stirrings of a theatre program," however, dramaturge Twyla Kitt says, took place in the Education Department, specifically in the On-site Programs Division, in which a staff

Charles Darwin, *performed by Eric Meyer. Photograph reprinted with permission of the Explora Science Center and Children's Museum.*

member with a theatre background realized that her task of developing theatre programs would be

easier with the support of a supervisor who also had direct experience in theatre and an understanding of the essential nature of theatre. At that time, the museum staff member who best fit this description was Barry Hayes, who was then Director of Multimedia Services. The creative skills and artistic vision of the multimedia staff dovetail nicely with the needs of a theatre department. They work with

The Brainiacs, *performed by Simon Hansen, John Michael Seltzer, and Gigi Dornfest.*
Photograph reprinted with permission of the Regents of the University of California.

scripts and actors, and convey concepts using visual elements, music, and narrative. They often present concepts through a story line that includes dialogue. Of
course, the department still relies on the support of the Education Department
for input into content selection and for review of scientific concepts, but grouping artists with similar goals in one department works quite well for the museum.

Public Programs

The Science Museum of Minnesota and the Lawrence Hall of Science both
established their theatre programs under the oversight of the Public Programs
Department. The theatre program of the Lawrence Hall of Science, however,
it is now part of the Large Groups Programs Department, under the umbrella
of Student and Family Programs.

WHERE WILL PERFORMANCES TAKE PLACE?

Professor Hans-Joachim Klein, of Germany's Karslruhe University, refers to performances that take place in galleries or exhibit spaces as "animated environments" or "living dioramas."

Adding live bodies, props, and sounds to exhibit spaces raises a number of concerns for exhibit planners, floor staff, and performers. Exhibit planners and floor staff need to consider that traffic patterns can be disrupted, and access to exhibits may be affected during performances. Performers need to be made aware that ambient noise and the comings and goings of visitors can be distracting not only for them but for visitors watching the performance. Ambient noise and movement can preclude quiet, moving moments of drama, and this places limits on the style of performances that can be presented in exhibit halls. Seating can also be an issue. Sight lines and comfort need to be taken into account, as does a measure of control. In spite of these challenges, museum theatre thrives on the context and content provided by exhibits, and much can be done to minimize the noise and distractions.

Suggestions for ways of delineating the performance area and the seating include lighting, stanchions, portable screens and awnings, carpets (which not only define the seating area but can also minimize noise), carpet squares for those comfortable sitting on the floor, and benches or stools.

Audiences unaccustomed to performances in museum spaces think nothing of strolling through the performance area. Extraordinary as it may seem, museum theatregoers occasionally do this even in a formal theatre space. Twice during performances in SMM's Science Live Theatre (an enclosed, formal theatre space, with raked seating, sound, and lighting), members of the audience entered and exited using the *back stage door* located *behind* the curtains and walked *between* the actors performing on the stage.

In Mellissa Marlowe's experience at the Witte, "museum galleries easily convert to performance space." She gives *Millie's War* as an example. This monologue was developed as

part of an exhibit to commemorate the anniversary of the U.S. entry into World War II. A large army tent was erected in the large, main first-floor gallery that served as part of the exhibit. This tent was written into the script of the play and the tent was instantly transformed into a small performance space six times a week. The performance transformed the otherwise boring tent into a lively topic of discussion and a vibrant performance area, truly allowing the audience to become a part of the play.

From 1996 until May 2000, all of the Carpenter Science Theatre Company's performances took place in gallery settings. Some of the challenges they faced have already been mentioned—acoustical and traffic problems, and poor sight lines. Partly for these reasons, in May 2000 a 119-seat theatre was inaugurated, consisting of a small thrust stage approximately twenty-two by fifteen feet, with a rear projection screen, stage curtains, some wing space, and a combination green room, storage room, and dressing room.

The Museo de Historia Natural performs exclusively in its gallery spaces, making every effort not to alter the physical spaces and to make the performances compatible with "the other tasks and functions carried out in the museum." All of their set and prop pieces are brought on for the performance and removed afterward. An upcoming play on AIDS will be the first performance in the museum's amphitheatre.

The Weisman has developed guidelines for performances in the galleries to prevent accidental damage to works of art. "We've also done a number of performances that move through the museum building and that use the Fiterman gallery that runs along the river," Colleen Sheehy says, adding, "We're game to try just about anything."

COORDINATING THEATRE ACTIVITIES WITH OTHER DEPARTMENTS
At the Science Museum of Virginia the performance group must coordinate their schedules with the Education, Visitor Services, and Marketing Departments, as well as with museum rentals and administration. As described by Larry Gard,

> Both the dramaturge/associate producer and the artistic director work with the Exhibits and Marketing Departments to coordinate the release of information about upcoming performances, as well as the production of signage for use in-house during a production run. The artistic director must work with the Facility Maintenance Department to accomplish the proper storage of Carpenter Science Theatre Company set pieces, costumes and props, in addition to making certain that the physical plant of the Eureka Theatre is maintained and, if necessary, repaired. For gallery performances, the artistic director must work with the Exhibits and Education Departments to decide on which location is the

best for performances to occur, and in establishing a performance schedule that does not conflict with the schedule of live demonstrations, which are performed in the galleries by Education Department staff members.

Buss reports that the Theatre and Outreach Program at Whitaker Center works with numerous departments within the center—as mentors to the youth volunteer program, to train docents, and as a tool for teachers and students in the Education Department.

As can be seen from these examples, museum theatre programs and personnel are versatile and can perform in a variety of styles and places; they can also share their presentation skills throughout the museum.

MUSEUM THEATRE AUDIENCES

Understanding our audiences is one of the keys to minimizing our frustrations with them and theirs with us. It is important to remember that visitors rarely come to museums to attend performances. Theirs is a different agenda, and museum theatre provides an unexpected experience. Not only have our audiences frequently not paid for the privilege of seeing a performance, but the performance itself, if it is on an exhibit floor, is surrounded by distractions. Also, if a museum is highly interactive, it is possible that audiences will see the performance in the same light as any other exhibit. They may not be aware that it would be desirable for them to modify their behavior by being quiet during the show, and by coming and going unobtrusively.

During a performance at the SMM of a piece on the religious significance of mummification, the actor placed a small salver on the floor and turned to enact a brief ritual with his back to the audience. When he faced front once more he found that his small audience had disappeared. He was understandably rather taken aback and not sure whether to continue the performance or not. In his confusion, he looked down, attempting to regain his composure. In the salver at his feet lay a five-dollar bill.

Understanding our audiences is not the same as catering to or accepting their every idiosyncrasy. It may seem incredible to some of us that most theatre performances nowadays are preceded by an announcement requesting that people turn off their cell phones. Isn't it obvious that ringing phones would disturb not only the actors, but the rest of the audience? Clearly it is not. In SMM's enclosed theatre space a preshow announcement is played requesting not only that people turn off their cell phones, but that they remain seated and limit their conversations to a minimum.

Performers need to be prepared for the fact that performing in museums resembles street theatre in many particulars; and they should receive support and training in how to handle difficult situations. That training needs to include an understanding of the institution's attitude toward heckling or any other behavior that affects the performance for the actors and for the audience. Zero tolerance is probably not an option, but neither is its opposite—total acceptance. There needs to be an agreed on point at which the performer may break character and stop the show if necessary in order to ask for adjustments in the audience's behavior.

One would expect that school groups would need the least guidance, accompanied, as they tend to be, by teachers and chaperones. My experience is quite the opposite. Families do the best job of monitoring behavior, schools the worst. At a recent performance of a show in which one performer was planted in the audience, gently questioning the theories on perpetual motion being expounded by an actor portraying an inventor, several teens in the front row were talking loudly and using the benches as recliners. The planted actor, who was sitting near them, was relieved to see a teacher leave the back row and approach them. It had become difficult for her to focus on her performance and hear her cues. It was not the teacher's intention to discipline the students, however; he headed straight for the actor (assuming she was a member of the audience) and proceeded to let her know how much she was "pissing him off." While this example is extreme, the fact remains that teachers frequently drop their students off at a performance and stand nearby holding conversations of their own, rather than monitoring behavior.

In order for a theatre performance to be successful, both the audience and the actors need to feel at ease. We can help audiences understand our expectations by telling them what those expectations are, and we can support performers by allowing them to take action when necessary.

Audiences may appear not to have registered any of the energy performers expend, but appearances can be deceptive. Veteran museum theatre performer Joan Lisi once told me that it was inevitably the person who had sat woodenly through her most heartfelt performances who walked up to her after the show, wrung her hand, and told her he had just had the most moving theatrical experience of his life.

NOTES

1. Zucker, "Anna Curtis Chandler: The Metropolitan's Costumed Storyteller," *Museum Theatre Journal* (Spring 1998).

2. Zucker, "Anna Curtis Chandler."

3. ASTC, *A Stage for Science* (Washington, DC: Association of Science-Technology Centers, 1979).

4. ASTC, *Stage.*

5. ASTC, *Stage.*

6. Judd, "Interactive Interpretation: Puppetry in Museums," *Museum Theatre Journal* (April 1993).

7. Paul Short, "The Magic of Puppets: Suspending Belief," *Museum Theatre Journal* (Spring 1997).

4

Selecting, Writing, and Developing Your First Program: From Fact to Fiction

ACT I

"We have a barn!" (Our institution)

"We have actors!" (Anyone will do)

"Let's do a show!" (Obvious conclusion)

ACT II

You find yourself in charge of your museum's first theatre production.

Whether or not you have any qualifications for undertaking this project is irrelevant. It's theatre! It's supposed to be good fun and you are clearly the person for *that* job!

ACT III

The education department is writing the script; volunteers have been found to make the costumes; the director of exhibits will move aside a few exhibit cases; and actors, as we all know, are a dime a dozen.

"But wait!" you say. "Who will . . . ?"

Here the list begins of all the tasks not considered by the well-meaning enthusiasts who put you in charge.

When I joined the staff at the Science Museum of Minnesota in 1984, the theatre program had been closed for two years due to funding restrictions. I made my entrance onto an empty stage and discovered that no one knew of anywhere else in the United States at that moment I could go to get an idea of how the museum theatre concept was being applied and practiced. Fortunately, this scenario is not likely to be repeated. Since 1984, not only have institutions of all types and sizes experimented with this technique, they have written articles about their experiences, held workshops about them, and many are willing to mentor newcomers.

Few institutions can devote resources to creating and funding a department focused only on theatre. Most museums, whether large or small, will utilize staff already responsible for other programs for their theatre venture. If funds *are* allocated for the project, they may be used to pay a producer and a director.

Whatever titles are used, someone needs to be assigned the overall organizational responsibility for the project. For the purposes of this chapter, that person will be called the *theatre coordinator,* or *TC,* and she will be female (saving us having to decide on *he, she, they, he or she,* etc.). The TC's main role will be to bridge the worlds of theatre and museums, and it will prove extremely helpful if she speaks the language of both. (The "green room" is the actors', not the environmentalists', hangout.) She will be doing a lot of mediating, whether the institution hires outside theatre groups to develop the production and stage it for them or those tasks are done in-house. It will be her task to help theatre people understand how her particular institution operates and vice versa. She will assist both groups to feel comfortable with their differences. She will guide the process from idea to production and may administer the budget. She may be asked to seek further funding, to hire those who will actually carry out the work of mounting the production, and to find volunteers when funds aren't available for salaries.

Apart from these responsibilities, she may also be asked to serve as *producer, director,* and *stage manager* for the new project. These are terms borrowed from the professional theatre world, in which they have very specific meaning. The producer, for example, is often in charge of raising the money required for mounting a production, and may or may not influence the artistic decisions. The director provides the overall artistic vision and directs the actors. He may leave before opening night and hand the show over to the stage manager, who typically ensures the smooth running of rehearsals and performances and is the person in authority in the absence of the director.

The responsibilities of these jobs can be merged in a variety of ways. In museum theatre, the producer and the theatre coordinator may be one and the same, as may the director and the playwright, or the actor and the stage manager. We will borrow the terms and use them *in ways applicable to museum theatre*, in order to focus on the tasks needing our attention. Situations and resources vary greatly, and tasks may be combined in ways I haven't even imagined.

Apart from identifying tasks, the purpose of this chapter is to assist TCs to articulate and anticipate what is involved in the production of a theatre piece, and thus to be better equipped to estimate the time and resources needed to accomplish the job. Whether your particular project is complex and involves large numbers of people, or very simple and involves only a few, the items listed here need consideration.

We will begin with the tasks that may fall to the TC, those of producer or stage manager. Those tasks include

- identifying the technical needs of the production and overseeing the hiring of technical staff such as set, prop, and costume designers;
- setting up auditions: placing audition notices, and planning the logistics of the auditions (including a plan of how to notify applicants regarding casting decisions);
- arranging for rehearsal spaces;
- acting as liaison between the artistic staff and museum staff, ensuring that the production of the theatre piece and its delivery to the institution is smooth;
- developing a plan for overseeing the production once it is up and running;
- arranging for evaluation, if this is part of the project;
- overseeing the dismantling of the production when it closes.

The TC needs to be prepared for the fact that actors will fill her life with drama—both while they are performing and when she wishes they wouldn't. They are storytellers, clowns, and pranksters rolled into one frequently unpredictable being. I don't know why I expected that actors would behave differently in a museum setting, but when I first undertook directing in a museum I was naive enough to suppose that they would feel as daunted as I did by the scholarship and the formality surrounding us. It was obvious to me that as a general rule museum people were not accustomed to unrestrained emotion, that they laughed nervously if certain four-letter words were dropped in their presence, and that they did not undress except in the privacy of their own homes. Most actors on the other hand laugh and cry quite comfortably in one another's presence, have what can only be described as an earthy vocabulary, and have few inhibitions about shedding their clothing. Even they, however, can sometimes cross the line with one another. Not long after I had hired my first group of actors, Heidi, a newly married performer, stormed in one morning and confronted Dan, an extremely handsome young man who often spoke before he thought. He had obviously done that the previous evening, because Heidi's husband had been nonplussed when he answered the phone and a rather anxious male voice asked, "Does Heidi have my jockstrap?" To Dan, this had been a very natural and innocent question. All five performers shared a dressing room and he assumed that Heidi, whose makeup table was next to his, had simply picked up some of his clothes by mistake and taken them home. Her husband hadn't seen it in quite the same light.

Try to imagine a similar situation arising between two of the curators at your museum and the gap that separates our two cultures becomes all too obvious, and the role of your TC all the more important.

■ ■ ■

Few museum theatre troupes can afford a person dedicated only to stage management. It is, however, a vital function. In traditional theatre, the stage manager is boss, often taking over the show when the director moves on to other projects. The stage manager organizes people and things, from calling rehearsals as needed to making sure that all the props are in working order.

In museum theatre, the role of stage manager is sometimes assigned to one of the performers. Performers may or may not have experience as stage managers, but professional actors appreciate and value good stage managers and are aware of their importance. They also know what function a stage manager serves. At the SMM performers stage manage their own shows. Their responsibility is primarily to report on breakages and buy supplies needed for the show. They are not expected to repair sets and props, except in the case of something minor, but do report problems to the technical manager or exhibit maintenance staff. Some shows have expendable or perishable supplies. The stage manager sees to it that supplies don't run out.

The stage manager will

- ensure that the rehearsal space is open and set up in a timely way, which may include bringing in furniture and props;
- oversee that actors arrive on time and warm up before the rehearsal begins;
- assist the director by keeping notes on blocking, script changes, or questions to be raised with designers;
- oversee the striking of items brought in for the rehearsal and which may need to be returned to other spaces;
- ensure that all set, prop, sound, and lighting equipment is in order before a performance begins;
- call extra rehearsals or line-throughs as needed after the show opens;
- dispose of sets, props, costumes after the show closes.

It is feasible for a performer to assume the role of stage manager (as per the SMM example). When making this choice, consider the following:

- What support will he/she have? Who else can be appealed to for help?
- Is he/she being given authority over the other actors and the technical staff?
- Is the actor being asked to do more than can reasonably be expected of a performer?

If, rather than separating these tasks, you choose to hire a producer/director, then you need to state clearly at the outset that you expect him to oversee the day-to-day planning of the production. If necessary, he will interview and hire technical staff, gather props, be responsible for setting up before and clearing after rehearsals, and run errands to collect set or costume pieces.

The director will

- provide the artistic vision and guidance for the project;
- audition and select the actors;
- approve the set, prop, and costume designs;
- conduct technical meetings as agreed on with the producer;
- conduct rehearsals;
- deliver a final product according to the deadlines agreed on with the producer;
- continue to supervise the project in accordance with the contract.

Directors can be hired to direct only or to direct and produce. Either way, their role is crucial. Even the best of plays and the most talented of actors can fail without a good director. Directors bring vision and focus to a project, they inspire actors to take risks and give of their best, and they are able to determine what may be the cause of a problem—the script, the setting, the process, an actor's personality or misunderstanding of a character. They make sure that sight lines are good, speech articulate, and blocking natural and comfortable for performers and audience alike. They coach when necessary, providing practical advice on acquiring an accent, or encouragement and support when a character is slow to develop. A play can conceivably do without a lighting designer or even a stage manager, but to a trained eye it is always obvious when a play has lacked direction.

If a director is only directing (not directing and producing), it is *not* his responsibility to seek out, hire, or supervise the technical aspects of a production—drawing up contracts, determining fees, signing purchase orders, overseeing deadlines. Although the responsibility for the overall final product is his, he will expect someone else (probably the TC) to perform such tasks as gathering the necessary props and making sure the rehearsal room is open.

■ ■ ■

It is not unusual for institutions to overlook some or all of the tasks detailed above when assigning responsibility for a museum theatre program, or when drawing up agreements with outside contractors. There are obvious logistical reasons why it is important to consider them—they are part and parcel of that organization and planning that helps to ensure a successful outcome. Beyond that is the less obvious cost in audience dissatisfaction and staff stress that can affect the institution in a variety of ways, from a letter of complaint about a promised performance that has been cancelled to the loss of valued personnel.

It is likely that you will find theatre folk reasonable, amenable to change, flexible, creative, cooperative, and honest—especially if you have carefully thought through what you expect of them, are willing to pay them fairly for it, and communicate your expectations clearly, and *in writing*. The importance of this cannot be overemphasized. The written contract demonstrates your professionalism and recognizes theirs. While a contract cannot cover every contingency, it can, when well crafted, protect all parties to it from gross abuse. If the contract states that the museum representative must approve costume designs before materials are bought and the costumes made, and this step is overlooked by the costumer who then delivers historically or ethnically inaccurate garments, the museum can refuse to pay for the work or to reimburse for the materials. If the museum approves the designs and then retracts its approval, the costumer may fairly claim payment and reimbursement.

■ ■ ■

The remainder of this chapter is devoted to playwrights, since the script development process elicits many questions and concerns. If you haven't recently revisited the question of *why* you want to do museum theatre, the moment when you decide to develop your first script is a good time to do so. Before any words are put on paper, it is also wise to consider *what* the goals are for your first project, and *who* will write the play. Quite frequently museums decide that the writing would be best done by an educator or a content specialist who is an expert on the subject. This is a common pitfall, or perhaps, to be consistent with our theme, pratfall. Writing a script is a craft, and playwrights are its practitioners.

While our audience may well include experts on the topic being presented, in all likelihood the majority of those watching a museum theatre play are either learning about the subject for the first time or being exposed to details they have not heard before. We want them to fall in love with the subject and continue to want to learn about it. Playwrights assigned a topic on which they are not experts will have to research it thoroughly before being able to write about it, and they will typically convey their knowledge in understandable, clear, and entertaining ways that reflect the process they themselves went through. Professional writers make their living by pleasing their audiences and their employers. You tell them what you want and they do their best to deliver it.

The question of content is frequently troubling for museum staff. Will the theatre people—playwright, actors, designers—care about the facts, or will they just be interested in the drama and sacrifice the content to effect? I often remind TCs that they are the determining factor in the process and there are no loose cannons. A script will not go into production that has not received approval. An actor will not invent material. A designer will not confuse the fifteenth with the nineteenth century. Why not? Because you will have monitored the process throughout, and, more importantly, because you are dealing with professionals whose aim is to serve you and the project you are jointly creating.

In an interesting reversal of the scenario many fear, I knew a playwright who found herself in the position of being the advocate for accuracy. She received a memo from the institution stating: "We obviously would prefer that (the script) be scientifically sound and logical in content, but frankly don't think being scientifically sound is as important as being engaging on issues that are critical." The playwright was in such profound disagreement with this approach that she resigned from the program.

HOW DO YOU FIND PROFESSIONAL WRITERS?

In the Twin Cities of Minneapolis and St. Paul, where SMM is located, we are very fortunate. We have three nationally recognized literary organizations—the Loft, SASE: the Write Place; and the Playwright's Center. All three groups are happy to let their members know that the Science Museum hires writers. If you live in an area without such amenities do not despair.

Step 1

An ad in the local paper is likely to produce many talented writers. Few writers make their living at this craft, they can therefore be found all over the country in communities of all sizes working at a variety of jobs. In placing an ad, be specific about your needs. "WANTED: Writer to develop a script for museum" will likely result in a deluge of responses from people with a vast range of abilities. I recommend modifying the following language:

Writer needed to develop a short educational script for museum theatre production.

Experience with playwrighting a must. (You can specify the level of experience required: must have taken writing classes; must have had a play produced.)

Experience with educational theatre desired.

Experience writing for young audiences desired or a must.

Demonstrated ability to work as part of a team desired or a must.

Stipend or pay commensurate with experience. (It is not necessary to state what the payment will be.)

For more information, please call . . .

or: Please send resume and letter of interest to . . .

A press release or announcement about the fact that your institution is looking for writers can also be sent to the English departments of local colleges and universities, and to professional and community theatres.

Step 2

How to Select from among the Applicants

You have placed your ad, sent out your announcements, and received ten responses. With the exception of the one who mangled the English language beyond recognition, the other nine are all promising candidates. What now?

- You write a polite letter of rejection to the language-challenged applicant, and call the others. You thank them for their interest and tell them that you want to see examples of their work. This would be a good time to describe your institution and the project for which they are being considered. Pay might come up, in which case you can give a range, explaining that it will depend on experience, the amount of time needed for research, and whatever other factors might influence the amount.
- You request a writing sample or samples, being specific about what you want. I recommend asking for at least two examples, no more than ten pages in length each. One should be a piece of writing about which the applicant is proud and that shows off his skills to their best advantage regardless of the subject matter. The other should be an example of a piece that required research and is factual in content. It could be about a historic event, a scientific discovery, a natural habitat, or politics. One of the two pieces should be an excerpt from a play.
- Indicate a deadline by which the material should be submitted.
- Writers are in the habit of sending a SASE—a self addressed, stamped envelope—for the return of their work. You will need to indicate whether or not you want this included.
- Give the writers an idea of when you will contact them, allowing at least four weeks after receipt of the material.

Step 3

Of the remaining nine, applicants one to five have responded within the time you specified. Applicant number six took himself out of the running after he learned what the stipend would be. The writing samples of seven and eight came in late. (Return the latter unread. You do not want to start off this way.)

Keep in mind that you are not being asked to judge the writing based on any criteria other than these: Does the writing please you? If it's meant to be funny, are you laughing? If it's meant to be moving, are you moved? If it's meant to be instructional, do you want to read on and be instructed?

In her thesis on the relationship between museum theatre and living history, Robin LaVoie has an excellent description of dramatic writing. It consists, she says

> of a series of discoveries, complications and reversals that lead the protagonist and the audience toward the ultimate conclusion. . . . Even performances only loosely based on a script or fully extemporaneous utilize the benefits of dramatic structure. . . . Every scene must have a beginning, middle and end, must involve high stakes and motivated characters and, above all, must *go* somewhere. This type of performance is quite different from simulating real life, because real life is full of moments when nothing happens.

LaVoie also quotes David Thelen as saying that a playwright explores the "tension between individuals and circumstances."[1]

Step 4

Choose your favorites from among the five and ask them to come in for an interview. It is advisable to have a job description available at this stage, one that can be mailed to the applicant before the interview.

The interview is your opportunity to find out whether this person, whose writing you have determined you like, can meet the requirements of this particular assignment. You will want to hear examples of other jobs the writer has done for hire, and of times when the writer has worked under conditions that resemble the ones he will face at the museum.

Here are some questions to ask in the interview:

- What do you think the main differences are between writing for the stage and writing for museum theatre?
- Have you ever written a commissioned play? (If yes, ask the writer to describe the situation.)

- Have you ever written a play based on factual material—a historical event, a real person, a place?
- Describe how you would prefer to work with content specialists, curators, educators. When and how do you want to hear their comments on your work?
- How would you approach writing for a special audience—preschoolers, families, women?
- Have you ever written for children?
- What do you think are the most important elements of a play written for _____ (fill in the blank—children, other special audiences)?

Close the interview by telling the applicant what to expect in terms of notification. Will you notify her by phone or mail, and within what time frame?

Step 5

You find yourself in a quandary. Three of the five applicants were not only enthusiastic about the project, they had all the necessary qualifications, and you know they would get along famously with everyone on the team. (You had serious doubts about the fourth, and the fifth called and cancelled the interview at the last minute.)

At this point, you can take one of two paths. Simply pick a candidate, knowing that the other two can be recalled in the future, or ask all three applicants to submit ideas for the project and then select one.

At SMM we invite playwrights to do this quite frequently. When assigning funds to the project, we include money—usually $600–$900—to cover the costs of two or three "treatments," (for a sample treatment, see appendix B). The unsuccessful keep their payments, and the amount paid to the successful playwright will be deducted from his or her total fee.

The applicants are given basic information about the subject matter to be covered in the play: number of actors we anticipate using, space where the play will be performed, target audience, length of the play, and budget for props and costumes. We then ask them to take a couple of weeks to come up with an idea of how they would present the topic. We ask them to write their idea out for us to consider, and then invite them to come in and talk to us about it in person.

Whether or not there is more than one writer competing for the job, a treatment is a good idea: it becomes the agreed-on base on which the writer will build. Reading it gives everyone involved in the project a chance to revisit and if necessary revise their assumptions and their goals before the writer actually starts writing the script.

Step 6

You should now be ready to select a playwright.

Step 7

The playwright delivers the finished product. Keep in mind that you have commissioned an artistic endeavor, and may therefore not receive exactly what you expected. It's possible that the play will not be to your liking. Should this happen, the only reason to withhold payment is if the writer has not fulfilled the conditions of the contract, or has written a text that differs widely from the agreed-on treatment.

If you decide to use the framework of the play with substantial alterations to the text, you are expected to pay in full. You are safe in utilizing the playwrights's ideas, so long as you abide by the conditions laid out in the royalties and copyright section of the contract. If another writer is hired to rewrite, then the question of joint copyright will need to be addressed. In the event of a sale of the script to another museum, will each writer receive an equal percentage of the royalties, or will they be shared? (If the play was commissioned as "a work for hire" this will not be an issue. See "Royalties and Copyright" below.)

Should you decide to start the process all over again, you will need to watch for unusual ideas proposed by writer A that might be considered her intellectual property. For example, she was commissioned to develop a play for preschoolers about the hydrologic cycle. She has developed a script utilizing the concept of two raindrops falling to earth and traveling through the cycle. You have determined that you like the idea, but the script itself is unacceptable. You pay writer A and proceed to hire writer B, who proposes a similar plot. The hydrologic cycle and how to explain it to preschoolers are not protected, but the characters of the two raindrops may be. The best approach is to discuss the situation with writer A, who may feel no attachment to the idea and consider that she has been paid for it anyway. She may ask for joint copyright, or may deny you the use of her concept. If the latter happens, it is probably not worth pursuing this any further. Send the new writer back to the proverbial drawing board to come up with an even better idea.

WHAT DO YOU PAY A PLAYWRIGHT?

Payment will depend on the writer's experience, the complexity of the play being developed, and the availability of the research. It will also depend on what writers receive for their work in your area, and on pay scales within your institution. The amount museums have paid writers varies widely from institution to institution, from a few hundred to several thousand dollars.

I do not recommend paying by the hour. Some writers are slow readers, and the research alone could run into the hundreds of hours before you know it. Also, while theatres pay playwrights a fee every time one of their plays is performed, I do not recommend a per-performance fee for museums. A flat fee should be agreed on for the project.

JOB DESCRIPTION AND CONTRACT

The job description should outline all the duties and responsibilities of the writer, from research to attendance at rehearsals. The contract should reflect the job description, with the addition of specified deadlines for accomplishing the tasks as outlined. It spells out when and how these duties and responsibilities are to be carried out, and outlines a schedule of payment based on job performance. It is common practice to pay half the fee on signing, and half on completion of the project. For playwrights, completion would be the point at which the final version of the play is handed in. It is important to examine expectations when writing the job description and the contract. Will the writer be expected to rewrite? How much, and when?

ROYALTIES AND COPYRIGHT

Museums typically hire writers in one of two ways. The museum contracts with a writer either for a work for hire, or for a work on which royalties are due. Under U.S. copyright law, original works written since January 1, 1978, are protected for the writer's lifetime and for seventy-five to ninety-five years thereafter. If you wish to be the sole owner of the commissioned work, your contract with the writer should state that this is a "work for hire." You will then be in complete control of the product and may sell it to others.

I recommend a joint copyright, with a contract stipulating that you have the right to produce the work indefinitely and may sell it to others, and a provision that states that if you do so, the writer will receive a percentage of the fee. Under joint copyright, the writer may also market the work to others. Should the writer succeed in this, the conditions should be outlined in the contract. A noncompete clause may protect you from having the work sold to another museum in your area that might choose to present it at the same time as you are presenting your own production. This is a highly unlikely scenario, but one that you need to be aware of in developing guidelines for working with writers.

I wish I could report that museums and their writers are getting rich from the proceeds of their work. Lamentably, this is not the case. Many museums do make their scripts available for others to use, and charge a fee. These sales are not frequent, and the amount of money involved is modest.

SMM charges $300–$600 for its scripts, a fee that entitles the buyer to produce the play for a year as often as it wishes. Should the buyer choose to charge admission to the play, no extra fees are due. SMM playwright contracts stipulate that the writer will receive 25 percent of the sale price.

Playwrights tend to prefer the joint copyright model because it resembles the royalty provisions of most plays, giving them a vested interest in the life of the play after their direct involvement with it is over. It also offers the possibility of future income, however modest.

USING ALREADY DEVELOPED SCRIPTS

There are two main categories of these scripts: commercially developed, often full-length plays, and scripts developed by museum theatre programs. Using commercially developed plays entails obtaining permission from the publisher of the play to produce the work, and a standard royalty agreement—a per-performance fee. Using plays developed by other museums is similar in that payment is usually expected, although it is rarely based on a per-performance fee. Permission is obtained directly from the institution.

Using other people's scripts is a smart choice for institutions wanting to test the use of theatre with a piece that has already been developed and proven successful. It simply requires an arrangement with the developers of the original material. A flat fee is usually charged, ranging from $400 to $700, and a contract is drawn up specifying what rights are being acquired.

As previously mentioned, at SMM contracts give the buyer of the script the right to produce it for one year. There are no limits on the number of performances that can be offered during that time, and the buyer is free to charge admission without any increase in the flat fee. The buyer agrees to credit SMM and the playwright on all publicity and written materials. No changes may be made to the script without the seller's permission. The kinds of changes that are frequently requested involve updates to factual information, cuts to the script, or the addition of regional information. These changes are submitted, in writing, to the seller, and approval is also obtained in writing for making the changes.

An example of such a sale was the script *Sara the Scientist*. Script rights belong to SMM and were acquired by the Cumberland Science Museum for $600. The play was presented to over nine thousand people at twenty-six schools, five adult organizations, two other museums, the Tennessee Parent Teacher Association, and the Cumberland Valley Girl Scout Council.

Examples of the use of existing full-length plays are the Strasenburgh Planetarium's production of *Galileo*, by Bertold Brecht, and the Oregon Museum of Science and Industry's production of *Nightfall*, by Isaac Asimov.

While the norm is to offer plays that relate to the institution, ASTC points out that "many science museums sponsor non-science theatrical programs to attract a new audience to the museum, or to fulfill their roles as community cultural centers."[2]

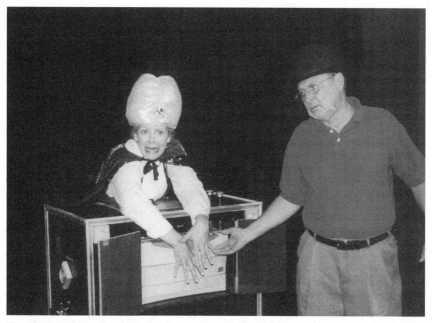

The Nature of Magic, *developed by the California Science Center, performed by Virginia Haggart and Richard Rousseau. Photograph reprinted with permission of the Science Museum of Minnesota.*

EXPERIENCES OF THE PARTICIPATING INSTITUTIONS

Science Museum of Virginia

At the Science Museum of Virginia, the process by which the subject of a script is chosen begins with a meeting between the artistic director of the Carpenter Science Theatre Company, the company's dramaturge and executive producer, and representatives of the Education and Exhibits Departments. This group examines upcoming exhibits and what scripts would best tie in with them, as well as what scripts might generate the most interest for the visitor. Educational content and entertainment value are discussed, as are practical considerations of time, budget, and technical requirements.

A content specialist is identified and assigned to the script, and the playwright is bound by contract to abide by all of the specialist's requests for changes and corrections to the factual information. Content specialists may be employees of the museum or outside experts.

Once the topic of a script has been decided on, the artistic director, dramaturge, and executive producer determine the length of the piece, the number of characters who will be appearing, the technical requirements, the overall tone of the piece, and the schedule for script development and production. The artistic director then selects a playwright and draws up a contract specifying deadlines for the first, second, and final drafts. "The contract," Larry Gard explains, "also specifies that the playwright has reviewed, and agrees with, the museum's creative process for the development of new scripts. It should be noted that the artistic director is given complete authority to approve or disapprove artistic elements of the script."

When the first draft is complete, it is submitted to the artistic director, who distributes it to the content specialist, the dramaturge and executive producer, and representatives from education, marketing, and administration. All feedback is given to the artistic director and the content specialist. The artistic director then meets with the playwright to discuss artistic elements, and with the content specialist to discuss factual content. Changes are made and a second draft prepared that undergoes the same process. Once a final draft is approved, the playwright participates in a workshopping process aimed at perfecting and finalizing the script before it goes into rehearsal.

The Science Museum of Virginia owns scripts in their entirety, and playwrights are paid per finished minute of script. For example, for a script requiring ten minutes to perform, a playwright would receive $1,500 to $1,800, or $150 to $180 per finished minute. There is a minimum fee of $1,200 for scripts less than ten minutes in length. Science Museum of Virginia scripts are available for use by other institutions for a royalty fee.

Science Museum of Minnesota

At the SMM ideas for new scripts come from a variety of sources—exhibit hall directors and their staff, volunteers, education and school services staff, grant writers, and public programs staff. These ideas may be connected to a particular grant or project, or relate to permanent exhibits and collections. Discussions take place between those who propose the idea and public programs staff. The desired outcome for the piece and the subject matter are examined, as is whether these ideas would be best served by a play or a demonstration. In the event that a play is chosen as the medium, we determine the target audience (for example preschoolers, teenage girls, adults, families) and where the play will be presented.

Two to three playwrights receive some basic information—the topic to be addressed, how many actors will be performing in the piece, what age it is intended for, where it will be performed, the desired length. (Additional, not essential, information could include a budget for set, props, and costumes.) Each playwright is then asked to develop an idea for approaching the play to be developed, and is given a deadline by which the idea needs to be submitted, in writing. This treatment consists of no more than two pages, and a sample is in appendix B.

The team selecting the playwright considers all the treatments and invites the writers in to present them in person and answer questions about them. One of the writers is then selected and his or her treatment amended to include requested changes.

Writers are paid a stipend of $200–$300 for the treatment and $1,500–$3,000 for the script. A contract is drawn up, including deadlines, a payment schedule, rehearsals the writer is expected to attend, and details of what the writer needs to include with the script—a bibliography, research materials that might prove useful to the performers, and so on.

From this point on, the writer's contact is with the director of public programs, who is the only person to receive the first draft. If the first draft is acceptable, it goes to the rest of the team for *content* review. If there are comments on the artistic merits of the script, they are given to the director, not to the writer. The director decides how, when, and if to pass these comments along. If the first draft does not meet the director's expectations, the writer prepares a second draft addressing the director's recommendations.

The Philadelphia Zoo Treehouse

When the troupe was first created, scripts were written by outside professional writers. As the troupe grew, in-house writers began writing shows, which become the sole property of the zoo.

The Treehouse regards scientific accuracy as a priority. "It is not an easy juxtaposition with the realm of theatre," Paul Taylor reports,

as there is often a fantasy component added when we begin to play animals. . . . I justify our use of anthropomorphism, as it is a useful tool for drawing a connection between our guests and the animals. We have established our own procedures for ensuring that all animal facts are correct. When we make assertions in shows that are factual, several people have scrutinized them.

These people include other Treehouse staff and the relevant animal expert.

Museo de Historia Natural

The Museo de Historia Natural begins its development process by conducting a bibliographic search on the chosen subject. After extensive study of the topic, the theatre team invites specialists in for a discussion. The play's objectives are determined, a plot is outlined, and the two writers on the team go to work developing a script. Scripts are reviewed by content specialists and by the program's mentor. Since the museum receives all of its funding from the state and does not charge admission, the question of royalties has never come up.

Carnegie Museum of Natural History

At the Carnegie Museum of Natural History scripts are written by staff with a writing or education background, assuring that the programming is "at the right level for the program audience and also that while fun and enjoyable, education is always of the utmost importance." Scientists and other museum staff review the scripts for accuracy of content. Goals for a program are set by the program specialist. "When a writer has been hired," Michael List says, "it is contractual. The contract states that the plays become property of the Carnegie Museum of Natural History. All of our plays are available to other institutions for a one-year period and a one-time fee."

Whitaker Center

At the Whitaker Center all programs are developed in-house "with our programming staff." George Buss writes that

> this begins in one of two ways. The first is a brainstorming session among upper management, when we develop possible ideas for new programs. The other is from a performance staff member who has an idea on a favorite exhibit or topic. In one instance, a staff member broke his leg, and some form of low-activity performance was needed to utilize this actor. After a brainstorming meeting, the idea was born to write a show on fractures and treatment, utilizing the X-rays from the staff member's own foot. From there a writer and a researcher are assigned. Depending on the size of the piece, this may be the same person. This is usually the Theatre and Outreach manager, though performance staff is often given writing projects like this. In the case of the fracture show, this job was given to the handicapped actor who then researched bone fractures and medical treatment. He wrote a treatment and outline for the show. This was reviewed by the Theatre and Outreach manager. After two more sessions together, they developed *No Bones About It*, a scripted conversation between visitor and actor with X-rays and demonstrations. . . . This was then reviewed by the vice president of the Science Center, the director of Exhibits and Programs, and the director of Education before being put on its feet (in a manner of speaking). Any idea or script that is created while working for Whitaker Center is the sole property of Whitaker Center. They are available for lease of performance rights for one year.

TIMELINE FOR SCRIPT DEVELOPMENT

(The actual dates are arbitrary.)

January 1–15	New idea for a play is discussed with the team and a basic concept is agreed on.
January 16–31	*Scenario A)* A playwright is chosen by the theatre coordinator and a contract prepared. A meeting is set up between the playwright, the team, and the theatre coordinator to discuss goals for the piece, responsibilities, and expectations. *Scenario B)* Several playwrights are identified by the theatre coordinator.
February 1–15	*Scenario A)* The playwright prepares a one-page treatment outlining the basic concepts to be explored in the play, its proposed length, location, age level, and number of characters. *Scenario B)* The playwrights are given information regarding the content of the play, its length, the age level they are writing for, where it will be performed, and the number of actors who will perform in it. They are asked to prepare a one- to two-page treatment outlining their ideas.
February 16–March 1	*Scenario A)* The treatment is reviewed, accepted, or rejected. *If rejected)* The playwright is paid for work done thus far and a new playwright is chosen, or the playwright is asked to prepare a different treatment. *If accepted)* The playwright is asked to prepare a first draft, or asked to amend the proposal. These amendments would not include changes to the original concept. *Scenario B)* Treatments are reviewed by the team, and the TC and playwrights are invited to elaborate on their ideas in person.

	All will be paid for their treatments. One will be selected and a contract drawn up for him or her.
April 30	The playwright submits the first draft.
May 1–15	The first draft is reviewed.
	If accepted) The playwright prepares a second draft, incorporating suggested revisions and corrections.
	If rejected) The playwright is paid in full if the conditions of the contract have been met. A new playwright is hired.
June 1–30	The play is rehearsed. The playwright is present as per the contract to make revisions.
July 15–31	The play opens for a trial run.
August 15	The playwright submits a final copy, incorporating changes made during the trial run.

ROLE OF THE TEAM

- To review or propose ideas for plays.
- To be available to answer the playwright's questions.
- To review and amend the content of the treatment submitted by the playwright.
- To attend rehearsals in accordance with guidelines established by the TC.
- To attend performances of the play.
- To be available to actors to answer questions.

The TC should discourage active team participation in rehearsals, especially early ones. With the exception of compliments, I recommend inviting the team to comment about the play only to the TC, not to the playwright or the actors. Putting a performance together is a balancing act, and poorly timed (however well-meant) criticism can derail this process.

NOTES

1. LaVoie, "To Engage and Enlighten: Theatre as an Interpretive Tool in History Museums" (master's thesis, Arizona State University, 2003); Thelen, "But is it History?" *The Public Historian* 22, no. 1 (2000), quoted in LaVoie, *To Engage.*

2. ASTC, *Stage.*

General Costs and How to Fund Them

There are as many examples of how to fund a theatre program as there are institutions that have succeeded in doing so. We will begin by addressing what the costs are, and then examine ideas for funding them.

COSTS

The first and largest cost of a theatre program is personnel. I am often asked why a theatre program could not operate entirely with volunteer labor. It could. If other areas of your institution are run by volunteers, then clearly this is an option for museum theatre as well. If, on the other hand, you employ professionals to curate your collections, design your exhibits, market your programs, and coordinate your educational activities, there is no reason to believe that you would want to run a theatre program any less professionally. This can be a surprising notion for museum administrators, and even for programmers. I was shocked to have a colleague comment to me recently that visitors at his institution would prefer to see a live program, even if the presenter was unprofessional and "dropped things," than no program at all. I challenge this theory on every level. It is true that audiences can be remarkably forgiving. At SMM one of our performers began a puppet show without the main puppet in place, an omission she did not become aware of until she reached for it and felt empty space. She stopped the show, asked the audience to excuse her, left the area to find the puppet, returned, and began the show again. No one left and no one complained. I would have been the first to support them if they had. There was no question, on the performer's part or on mine, that this was "okay."

It is not necessary to hire presenters who are considered professional by commercial theatre standards, only presenters who aspire to meet or surpass those standards, and whose supervisors will provide them with all the training and direction they will need to do just that.

Salaries for theatre professionals vary tremendously from area to area of the country (and even within states), and according to the level of expertise of those you hire. One simple and straightforward way of determining rates of pay for your area is to call various theatres (particularly educational theatre groups) and ask them to give you a salary range for performers and technical personnel. It is advisable to inform yourself about the highest and the lowest salaries being paid by including professional, top-of-the-line theatres in your research, as well as smaller theatres. Once you have an idea of what the salary range in your area is, you can offer a competitive salary that is fair both to your budget and to the people you will hire.

What follows is a list of the personnel necessary to mount a theatre production. Some of these functions can be blended with others (a set designer may also design and build props, an actor may perform a piece he has written, etc.), and some functions might be carried out by existing museum personnel. My purpose in listing them is to cover the *tasks* that *someone* must perform in order for a play to be produced. (Details regarding these functions have been covered in chapter 4 for playwrights and will be reviewed in chapter 7 for the others.)

Playwright

Producer

Director

Costume Designer/Builder

Set Designer/Builder

Prop Designer/Builder

Actor(s)

Stage Manager

Other technical requirements could be lighting, sound, or special effects.

Whether you will hire out each of these tasks or not, the following exercise is useful for determining the amount of staff time that will need to be devoted to a theatre production. For example, it is important when considering salaries to include preparation and meeting time. It is not sufficient, when budgeting, to count only those hours spent actually performing or writing.

Playwrights

Factors to consider in budgeting for a playwright's salary include the following:

- Number of hours the playwright will be expected to spend in meetings with content specialists, education staff, and anyone else who may have a say in the content or style of the production
- Range of hours that will be spent doing research; for instance, twenty to thirty-five
- Number of rehearsals the playwright will be expected to attend
- Number of hours allocated for rewrites not included in the initial contract—this covers unexpected contingencies outside the scope of the contract
- Number of performances the playwright will be expected to attend

Factors determining the playwright's pay rate include writing experience, complexity of the research, and the length of the play.

Producer

Factors to consider in budgeting for a producer's salary include the number of hours allocated for the following:

- Tasks such as placing audition notices, hiring technical staff, supervising the production process, and payroll
- Meetings with the director, playwright, designers, and museum staff

- Wrapping up the project. Will the producer be in charge of determining the distribution of props, costumes, or items acquired for the production into storage or other areas?

Director

Factors to consider in budgeting for a director's salary include the number of hours allocated for the following:

- Meetings with the producer, playwright, designers, and museum staff
- Reviewing resumes, conducting auditions, and contacting actors (contacting actors and making job offers might fall under the producer's responsibilities)
- Preparing for rehearsals
- Rehearsing
- Contingency funds should also be available in the event that the director has to be recalled for recasting or redirecting

Designers—Set, Prop, and Costume

Factors to consider in budgeting for designers' salaries include the following:

- Number of hours the designers will spend meeting with the producer, playwright, actors, and museum staff
- Cost of the designs
- Number of hours the designers will spend building the set, props, or costumes
- Number of rehearsals the designers will be expected to attend
- Hourly rate for repairs or remaking of items in the event of breakages, cast changes, and so on
- Hourly rate for maintenance during the run of the performance

Actors

Factors to consider in budgeting for actors' salaries include the following:

- Rehearsal hours the actors will be expected to attend
- Hours assigned to research and memorization
- Hours estimated for costume fittings
- Performances the actor will do

In addition, contingency funds should be available for extra rehearsals and performances.

If a rehearsal is scheduled from two to four o'clock it is recommended that you count the actors' time as one to five o'clock. Actors need time to warm up, change clothes, review lines, and set props. At the end of the day, time is also needed to reverse the process (with the exception of unlearning their lines)—to change clothes, put away props and set items, and, in most museum situations, check in with museum staff about the project. The same estimate needs to be made for performances.

Stage Manager, Lighting, Sound, and Special Effects

It is unusual for a museum to hire these functions out separately from one of those already listed—commonly, the set designer will also determine the lighting requirements, and one of the actors may be assigned stage management duties.

Not covered here are indirect costs, which you may be asked to estimate. These can include space use, space maintenance, utilities, and staff time not listed above. Staff that might be asked to report time spent on theatre programs can include reservations, floor staff, curators, and educators.

FUNDING

Federal Grants

Federal funding can be sought from three major agencies:

The National Science Foundation (NSF)

The most successful applicants to NSF have included funds for theatrical programming within a bigger exhibit or program grant. NSF typically does not consider funding personnel, such as paying an actor's salary, but it has funded development and production costs. Information can be accessed through the NSF website (simply enter *National Science Foundation* in a search engine) or by calling the NSF at 703-292-8210. The foundation also conducts outreach on proposal preparation.

The National Endowment for the Humanities

Similar criteria apply as for NSF. Their website is also easily accessible, and their telephone number is 202-606-8500.

The National Endowment for the Arts (NEA)

The NEA funds a wide variety of artistic activities, including writing and performing. Their website is well laid out and easy to access. Their telephone number is 202-682-5400. The Walters Art Gallery in Baltimore, Maryland, received a grant in 1986 from the NEA. The purpose of the grant was to fund interpretation of the Walters's late Gothic works of art. As Diane Brandt Stillman describes it, "Using objects from the Walters's outstanding collection of late Gothic secular objects (ivory jewelry casket, salt cellar, gingerbread mold, and chess box)" the actor portraying a sixteenth-century lord of the manor "discussed leisure pursuits, dining habits, and game playing while pointing out the artistic features of each object. After the lord left to fetch his lady for prayers, the Franciscan friar greeted the 'pilgrims' and welcomed them to the 'chapel,' where he eloquently explained the scenes of the Passion on a great oak altarpiece."[1]

The Department of Education

Funds may be available under Title II for professional development activities whereby state agencies of higher education may make partnership grants to institutions of higher education and nonprofit institutions, including museums. These grants could be developed to cover an educational partnership between a school and a museum to develop and present educational theatre.

State Funding

State funding varies dramatically from one area to another. Some state agencies can be approached to fund special projects. Environmental or water boards, for example, have been known to subsidize the production of programs that will include information important to them and that complement their mission. Some states have arts boards and issue grants through them. At the Science Museum of Virginia, the state funds the salary and benefits of the Carpenter Science Theatre Company's artistic director.

Private Funding

Foundations, corporations, local businesses, and individual donors have been among the major sources of funding for museum theatre programs.

The Pittsburgh Children's Museum (PCM) has been extremely successful in obtaining private funds. Describing how this came about, museum director Maggie Forbes wrote that "the most dramatic—literally as well as figuratively" —impact of their puppet exhibit Mystery, Magic, and Mirth was the introduction of performance-based programming.

> During the first few months after the opening the staff heard only one consistent complaint: puppet shows were regularly sold out. The museum's first response was to increase the price of tickets from 50 cents to $1.00. Next it scheduled more performances. Then it hired a second puppeteer. Eventually it built a larger theater. Finally the PCM embraced a whole new direction in programming: multifaceted quarterly themes exploring a single topic, each with a performance centerpiece.[2]

With this success under its belt, the PCM went on to produce *The Adventures of Corporal Corpuscle*—

> a rollicking musical adventure story in which "Fruit of the Loom"–style organs unite to battle off the menacing Gooky Green Germ. . . . In the spring of 1987, after its 12-week run at the museum, "Corporal Corpuscle" won the first Health Education Award from a subsidiary of Blue Cross/Blue Shield. Reluctant to see the play close, the PCM successfully applied for funding from the Allegheny County Medical Society to adapt the play to a touring show. . . . In its six months of travel, the play was enjoyed by more than 20,000 students. Educators responded with rave reviews.

Shortly afterward, the museum "received a two-year grant from the Howard Heinz Endowment to hire actors and a schools/outreach coordinator."[3]

The Science Museum of Virginia's Carpenter Science Theatre Company is funded by private grant monies. The only exception is the artistic director's salary and benefits, which are funded by the state. Since the company was founded in 1995, it has received approximately $860,000 for production expenses and capital expenditures from the E. Rhodes and Leona B. Carpenter Foundation. Eighty percent of the funds have been devoted to production expenses, and 20 percent to equip the Eureka Theatre within the museum.

The Science on Stage program at the Carnegie Museum of Natural History was initially funded by CNG, a local natural gas company now owned by Dominion Natural Gas.

The Whitaker Center for Science and the Arts funds its Big Science Theatre out of its general operating budget, but some shows are underwritten by sponsors, such as their *Trash or Treasure* show, which

> had its development costs underwitten by the Pennsylvania Department of Environmental Protection in 2000. In 2003, this same show was underwritten again by Waste Management of Central Pennsylvania to stage a revival of this recycling show. Another show, *Super Cold Science*, was underwritten by Green's Premium Ice Cream, while *Magic Numbers* was underwritten by Amp Tyco Corporation. The Kunkel Foundation of Harrisburg gave one year's support to the program in 2001. . . . Whitaker on Wheels is primarily funded by a grant from the Whitaker Foundation Regional Program administered by the Greater Harrisburg Foundation, including personnel and materials, as well as funding the purchase of the Whitaker on Wheels van. Brenner Dodge sponsored the van, covering the cost of all maintenance for it as it travels the many miles for outreach. Fifty shows of Great Food Pyramid were underwritten by Mid-Atlantic Dairy Association to spread the word about good eating habits.

Explora received three grants of $50,000 each in 1993, 1999, and 2001 from the Urban Enhancement Trust Fund of the City of Albuquerque to fund its Teaching Through Theatre—the Great Artist, Scientist, and Explorer Series. The Urban Enhancement Trust fund is a permanent fund used to subsidize cultural services projects. The grant specified that Explora could not charge admission to the play, so the museum established free days on the Saturdays when the plays were being presented. "A strong increase in attendance!" was reported.

The Lawrence Hall of Science has received grants from the Alameda County Recycling Board, the Contra Costa Water District, the San Francisco Recycling Program, the California Air Quality Board, and the Tobacco Control Section of the California Department of Health Services.

SMM includes the costs of its theatre and demonstration programs in its general operating fund. For the initial start-up costs incurred over thirty years ago, the Louis and Maud Hill Foundation gave the museum a $45,000 grant and the State of Minnesota put in $144,000 to be spread out over two years. Personnel costs have been covered in a variety of ways. Initially, the Bremer Foundation funded a five-year internship for college and university students. In later years, the theatre program was able to access approximately $100,000 in funds through the Comprehensive Employment Training Act, by hiring actors and playwrights who were learning their respective crafts. The Job Training Partnership Act for high school students allowed the SMM to employ students for three months during the summers to assist in administration, prop gathering, and costuming.

Costs for individual productions were underwritten by the Pollution Control Agency, the Minnesota Computer Consortium, Beverly Enterprises (nursing homes), and the Northwest Area Foundation, which funded the hiring of a Native American actor for a special presentation. SMM has applied for and received exhibit development grants from both the National Endowment for the Humanities and the National Science Foundation. Included in these grants have been requests for funding accompanying programs.

Sponsors

The Whitaker Center for Science and the Arts has used its contacts within the community to build partnerships and sponsorships with the following:

- The Mid-Atlantic Dairy Association, which funded a script about the food pyramid and fifty performances in area schools.
- The International Institute for the Advancement of Medicine, which donated human body organs to be used in the demonstration *Bodyworks,* about organ donation.
- Gift of Life, Pennsylvania's organ and tissue donor program donated a "Stuffee" doll, "a nine-foot-tall, blue-haired, interactive friend whose insides can be pulled out as teaching tools."

Fees

Additional fees are sometimes charged for viewing a theatre performance. Ticket prices depend on other comparable fee-based programs offered by the institution, the length of the program, and production values and professionalism. During the summer of 2002, SMM had the touring Science of Illusion exhibit developed by the California Science Center, with its accompanying magic show, a two-person presentation featuring a magician and an actor posing as an audience member who becomes part of the show. To test the revenue potential of live programs in a one-hundred-seat theatre, a $1 surcharge was added for the show. It consistently sold out. Taking the experiment one step further, the marketing department decided to double the ticket price to $2. Once more, there were no complaints and the show continued to sell out.

Outreach programs can, and usually do, command a fee. Again, the price depends on the same criteria applied to in-house programs, taking into consideration what schools typically pay for comparable programs. Generally speaking, the fee should cover the direct costs of transporting the program, and actors' salaries if they are hourly or contract workers. When the museum can count on ongoing bookings, the fees often cover all the costs of the program.

NOTES

1. Diane Brandt Stillman, "Living History in an Art Museum," *Journal of Museum Education* 15, no. 2 (Spring/Summer 1990).

2. Maggie Forbes, "Museum Theatre in a Children's Museum," *Journal of Museum Education* 15, no. 2 (Spring/Summer 1990).

3. Forbes, "Museum Theatre."

6

There's an Actor
in Our Collections!

In the case of the SMM, this is literally true. Our venerable puppets, Pete and Doc, the first ever to perform at our institution, do indeed reside in our collections vault.

Due to a generalized mistrust in the stability of artists in general and performers in particular, it is not unusual for museum staff accustomed to dealing with the strictures of academic research and scientific accuracy to ask themselves what will happen to the information they have so rigorously arrived at when it is placed in the hands of actors, directors, designers, and other highly imaginative folk. Will we suddenly hear Charles Darwin holding forth in rap, or the Pythagorean theorem explained as a new age mantra?

A little-known fact outside the theatrical profession is that actors who remain gainfully employed are among the most disciplined and flexible of beings. They have to be. Lateness is not tolerated in the theatre, and you are expected to perform unless it can be proved that you have actually died (preferably on the job). There are hundreds of applicants for every opening, most of whom, an actor always suspects, are more talented than he is. At auditions an actor will be asked to do things most of us would sooner die than do in public—such as singing, crying, or pretending to be inanimate objects with complex feelings.

Actors bring a wonderful depth of emotion and commitment to their portrayal of characters, as those who saw the movie *Tootsie* may recall. In it,

Dustin Hoffman plays an actor desperate for work. When he is being considered for the part of a tomato in a commercial he becomes so involved with his role that his agent threatens never to send him out on an audition again.

The *Pittsburgh Post-Gazette* described an actor "in the eminent and established Three Rivers Shakespeare Festival as 'otherwise and better known to thousands of school children as The Pittsburgh Children's Museum's dastardly Gooky Green Germ!'"[1]

So how are we to ensure that if asked to portray Albert Einstein the actor will not make up his own version of that eminent scientist's life? We need to go back to the moment when we decided that Albert Einstein was a good idea. At that point, we articulated our reasons for choosing this particular subject, and, as outlined in the chapter on developing scripts, we established certain goals for the piece and assigned the writing to someone who provided a script for our review and approval.

This script has been given to the actor, and he has been told to memorize it. This is second nature to an actor. Some, it is true, are more meticulous than others, but if our actor is the professional we know him to be, he is well aware that there will be times when he will work for directors who do not tolerate one word out of place. So far, so good. The actor has a script, and he is not expected to deviate in any substantial way from it.

Being a pro, he will also do a lot of research, which will undoubtedly be part of his contract with your institution anyway, knowledge of his character's history being an integral part of his commitment to you. He may even discover facts about Einstein that the playwright didn't discover or deliberately omitted, and feel tempted to include them. That's where personal discipline, a clear relationship with museum staff, and supervision come in.

Having said all this, we need to be prepared for situations in which the actor finds the temptation to improvise irresistible. At SMM we perform a piece called *Principles of Perpetual Motion.* In it, an actor plays an inventor displaying a perpetual motion machine. During the course of the presentation, another actor, a plant in the audience, brings up the laws of thermodynamics and questions the premise that any machine can do what the inventor claims. At the end, the plant walks out.

Audience reactions to this piece have been a study in gender politics. The degree of playfulness or aggression and confrontation (always kept to a minimum) depends on who plays which part. We have discovered that our audiences are very uncomfortable with a male plant and a female inventor. In this case, the plant must be very gentle and humorous not to arouse the audience's ire. One of our male plants once left the theatre to find that three male audience members, all much larger than he was, had followed him and wanted to know what he thought he was doing "harassing the lady."

Two females, or two males, can engage in some fairly heated argument without any negative audience reaction, and a female can question a male and even receive audience support in some cases. (One of the goals of the piece is to get the audience to raise objections and bring up the physical laws that make perpetual motion impossible.)

One of our combinations consisted of a veteran museum theatre actor and a new female plant. The show went very well, with a lot of audience participation. When the time came for the plant to depart, she did so, but popped back for a final parting shot. "By the way," she told her partner, "your fly is open."

What if you want to use nonactors as performers? As I have already stressed, I believe that theatre productions in museums should be treated with the same attention the institution gives to its other functions. The reasons

The Many and Wondrous Adventures of Splish and Splash *by Marilyn Seven, performed by Leslie Oremus and Tara Trooien. Photograph reprinted with permission of the Science Museum of Minnesota.*

given for wanting to use volunteer performers are typically financial. Theatre is fun, and it is not difficult to find people willing to participate in it. Since the choice to use nonprofessionals is quite frequently made, this chapter will begin and conclude by offering examples of institutions that have done so.

HIRING NONACTORS

In 1990, the Monterey Bay Aquarium hired marine biologists trained in interpreting natural phenomena to add theatrical techniques to their presentations. It is important to note that the biologists were not being asked to *act*, only to augment their presentations with theatre techniques that included audience interaction and participation, and the use of props. Patricia Rutowski, who was the aquarium's coordinator of Outreach Education at the time, explained that sometimes theatre professionals were brought in to assist with training or to direct a program.

During the early 1990s, the Please Touch Museum in Philadelphia adapted folk tales and presented plays on conflict resolution and fantasy adventure shows for their audience of children aged seven and younger. As Barry Szeig, theatre director of Touch Tales, described in the Fall 1995 issue of the *Journal*,

> We formed our very own children's theater troupe to create and produce our own theater shows designed for young children and their parents. Now you might wonder, who comprises our highly energized theater troupe? High school students of course! We bring together some of the most talented and brightest teenagers in Philadelphia to create and write original children's theater productions. Our troupe, the TOUCH TALES, is an ensemble troupe specializing in interactive children's theater for kids ages seven and younger. Our unique students come from three Philadelphia public high schools. . . . All the students audition and participate in an acting, writing, and directing internship, dedicating their weekends and afternoons at the Museum to rehearse and perform.[2]

David Hutchman, the current theatre experience manager at Please Touch, says that the program is still spoken of in glowing terms.

Hutchman's own experience with using high school students was not as positive as his predecessor's. During his first year at the museum, he developed a performance program using students from the High School for the Creative and Performing Arts (CAPA). "We targeted CAPA thinking that if anyone would be trainable it would be students who had chosen acting as their future profession." Three plays were mounted during a four-month summer season, all written, directed, and stage managed by Hutchman. Museum administrators believed that "it would be a wonderful idea to have 'community children performing for the museum children.'" Budgets were tight, and money could be saved by not paying professional actors. (Students received rehearsal pay and $25 a day for three performances.) The hope was also expressed that the program would lighten Hutchman's own performance schedule. His instincts told him otherwise, but while he had a wealth of children's theatre experience, none of it was in a museum, and Hutchman did not trust his instincts "about where this high school program should fit into my overall program. I was being told (by more experienced museum professionals with no theatre experience) that it should be easy, and even though in my heart of hearts I knew better, I tried to oblige."

Past experience had taught Hutchman that "performing for children is incredibly challenging, a true test of one's performing instincts and skill and ultimately very rewarding." What he learned from his experience utilizing high school students was

that subtlety and even the most basic of stage techniques were not my young actors' forte. Energy galore, yes. But trying to keep that energy under control while holding the arch of the story intact *and* making the program accessible to our young-young audience *and* being able to do it consistently were hard-fought-for items on my director's agenda. The students simply had no training for this kind of work. And I had no intention of dumbing things down to suit their craft level. Their assumption, and one that was unfortunately reinforced by their school, was that children's theatre was loud and fast and people fell down a lot. Perhaps the most damaging aspect was that they also saw the whole project as just something to do until they became big stars.

As for easing his schedule, Hutchman "ended up being here every time the kids were in the building and my weeks soon stretched into six and seven days. I was simply doubling my work instead of easing it."

By the time they were halfway through their second production, "lateness and absenteeism became such a problem that there were days when we had to rewrite the show on very short notice from five actors down to two. The students simply did not understand that this was a professional job and should be treated as such." None of them had ever performed in a show that ran for more than three performances, and they did not seem interested in acquiring the skills necessary to keep a performance fresh, consistent, and focused. "Eventually, despite phone calls to confirm performance dates and reminders of pay, there came a day when only one actor showed, and performing was simply impossible."

The Minnesota Zoo used volunteers for its Zoo Theater. The project was the brainchild of volunteer Grant Spicklemier, who had a theatre background and was a biology major at Bethel College in Saint Paul, Minnesota. He sent letters and flyers to college drama departments and local theatres, and placed an ad in the audition section of the *Minneapolis Star Tribune*. From the twenty-three people who auditioned, Spicklemier assembled two casts and created the volunteer force known as "Theater in the Wild Players." Performances were presented on Sunday afternoons and played to standing-room-only crowds.

Another institution that relied on volunteers was the Hidalgo County Historical Society (HCHM). As Oliver Franklin, former education officer for the society, reports in the spring 1996 edition of the *Journal*, the Drama Department of the University of Texas, Pan American,

> offered rooms for rehearsals and auditions, and practicum hours to participating student volunteers. . . . A local playwright provided two scripts gratis. . . . University students made up the actors and dressed them in costumes they had sewn themselves. . . . Despite kooky missteps, like the discovery that the salt trader's coat sleeves had been sewn on upside down, the day was a smash hit with favorable reviews. . . . The local public television affiliate filmed the plays for broadcast. Schools sent their children in on Saturdays. The entire program cost HCHM a grand total of $150.

At the Weisman, university students often perform in plays, and sometimes create an entire piece, writing, directing, and acting in it.

The benefits of using volunteers include reduced cost, community and student involvement, and the presentation of programs that might not have been created in any other way. The challenges are also clear. They include scheduling difficulties, varying degrees of commitment and discipline, and varying quality.

HIRING PROFESSIONALS

What I mean when I use the words *professional actor* is a performer who has sought vocal, movement, and acting training, whether in a full-time, a part-time, or a private capacity; and who brings professional standards to his work—punctuality, responsibility, and a positive attitude. I do *not* use the words to mean *only* actors who are members of Equity (the actors' union), or who have received payment for their work.

What sets the professional apart is training, experience, and salesmanship, characteristics that should be evident from the actor's resume.

Training

The actor's resume will contain information on where and by whom the actor was trained in his craft. This training includes voice, movement, acting, and sometimes other special skills such as dance, mime, puppetry, and music. The resume may also list private classes with well-known coaches, or workshops attended by the actor.

Experience

The resume will list productions the actor has been in and what part he has played in them. This will give you an opportunity not only of seeing what the actor has done, but of observing a career path. Perhaps you will notice that this actor has chosen to perform in more than one educational or children's theatre performance.

Salesmanship

A professional actor will typically have invested time and effort in his resume, in his "head shot" (photograph), and in presenting himself to you in the best possible light. If he has received professional training it will have included audition coaching. You will see a well-prepared audition focused toward your needs, and a well-groomed and appropriately dressed actor presenting it.

HOW DO I FIND PROFESSIONAL ACTORS?

Much depends on where you live. Clearly, a large city with an active arts community will be richer in professional actors than one offering little or no theatre. (Suggestions for the latter will be included at the end of this section.) There are several places where notices can be placed advertising the fact that you are looking for actors. The first is the newspaper. Some papers even have an audition section. Some communities offer online services for theatre work. Other sources are professional and community theatres, universities, and colleges.

It is important that your ad or press release answer the following questions, some of which are considered illegal at worst or politically incorrect at best in other job categories:

- Are you looking for male and female actors? (In my opinion it is regrettable that the word *actress* is going out of use. Theatre was one of the few professions in which women had achieved the distinction of their own title, and it was useful in placing notices. Nowadays one sees the redundant *male actor* or the grammatically challenged *female actor.*)
- Is age important? If you know that you only need two actors who can pass as teenagers or one actor who needs to play a seventy-five-year-old woman, say so.
- What is the time commitment (e.g., five days a week for ten weeks; summer only, part-time; full-time salaried)?
- Is this a paid position? (You do not need to specify the amount at this point.)
- Where should actors call to make an audition appointment?

It is wise to include a brief description of the work:

Actors wanted to perform in short educational plays for history center.

Actors wanted for outreach performances to primary schools.

If you are in a community with few theatre resources you will need to expand your search to the nearest city or college, keeping in mind that performers are often willing to travel, especially if yours is a seasonal program and your community is willing to offer housing free or for very little cost.

AUDITIONS

Actors get work by means of auditions. The audition doesn't take the place of an interview, but is a preliminary to it. The purpose of the audition is to determine whether a person can act. You may be surprised by the number of people showing up at your auditions who can't.

Prior to placing the notices you will need to decide the following:

- Where will the auditions take place?
- Who is going to conduct the auditions? This is typically done by the person who will be directing the play. If this person is not a museum employee, the theatre coordinator may wish to be present.
- What will you ask actors to bring to the auditions? A head shot? A resume?
- Will you have a form for them to fill out? (See appendix E.)
- How much will you be paying for the work?
- What do you want the actors to prepare? (See below.)
- At what time do you want the actors to arrive?
- Are there special considerations at your institution for reaching the audition space?
- How will you notify auditioners of your decision? By telephone? Mail?
- Will each actor audition alone or in a group with other actors?
- A job description (see appendix D) and a schedule of rehearsals and performances should be made available at the time of the auditions.

Most of this information will need to be conveyed to the actor when he calls for an appointment. At that time, you will explain what you want him to do for you.

I recommend asking the actor to prepare two pieces, total running time not to exceed five minutes. (One can be longer or shorter than the other.) The first piece should reflect the actor at his best. It can be a piece in any style and from any time period, comic or tragic. The second piece should be interactive, including the audience (usually the group with whom the actor has auditioned) in some activity. This gives you an idea of how the actor handles audience interaction, deals with unforeseen occurrences, and responds to right and wrong answers to his questions or instructions. It also gives you an opportunity of seeing the other actors in the group for a third time, doing something they haven't prepared.

Sometimes, actors have difficulty understanding what you want from them in the interactive piece, so giving examples can be helpful—"you can teach us a song or an activity"; "tell us a story that requires participation from us." This can result in highly entertaining and unusual presentations. I have been treated to the sight of a condom being placed on a broom handle, the reading of the Sunday ad supplement, the making of salsa, and the repair of a toilet.

Additional activities that can be added to the audition include the following:

- "Cold readings"—reading from a script that the actor has not seen before
- Guided improvisation—performers are given a theme, or story
- Activities that meet the special needs of the piece, for example, movement, music, gymnastics

If you are grouping actors for auditions, the person conducting them needs to prepare to make an opening and a closing statement. The opening statement should be as brief as possible and be limited to a welcome and outlining procedures: What order will the actors go in? May they use what's in the room during their presentation? The closing statement should thank them for their participation, ask if there are any questions, and inform the group of how and when they will hear of your decision.

AFTER THE AUDITIONS
Select the number of people you want to call in for an interview. Decide ahead of time what questions you will ask—questions that will help you to obtain more information about the person's experience, qualifications, and suitability for the job. Once you have selected the person you want, contact the others. (At SMM we return resumes and head shots.) Some of the applicants are people you might want to call back in the future; feel free to tell them so and keep their materials on file.

HOW MUCH TO PAY ACTORS
One of the best ways to arrive at equitable pay is to call around to as wide a range as possible of theatres or institutions that hire actors and ask them to share their salary range with you. That will give you an idea of what actors will expect to earn if they are employed at the largest and most prominent local theatre, and also at the smaller companies. In all likelihood, museums will fall somewhere in between. It is also important to take into account what the salary ranges are within your institution and not deviate too far from them.

UNIONS
There are various unions to which professional actors can belong. *Actors Equity* represents stage actors. *AFTRA*, the American Federation of Television

and Radio Artists, represents performers who work in radio, television, video, voice-overs, animation, and other recordings. *AGVA*, the American Guild of Variety Artists, represents performers who work in theme parks and other venues such as cabarets. Union rules apply to you only if your institution is what is called a *union house*, in other words an institutional member of that union. I know of no museum that is.

Actors who belong to these unions can be adversely affected by going to work for nonunion houses, but rarely if the purpose is educational. There are several exemptions available to actors who wish to do nonunion work. One is the educational exemption, which most museums fall under. In another, a union member notifies her union that she wishes to become a "financial core" member. This declaration must take place, in writing, before a nonunion contract is signed.

Union representatives are available for consultation and to offer guidance should a union actor be concerned about accepting employment with you. I recommend that the actor be the one contacting the union, not the museum.

WHAT ACTORS NEED

Actors need space for rehearsals—space that is clean, quiet, and fairly large, depending on the number of actors and the shows being rehearsed. They also need a changing or dressing room, a secure space where they can leave their clothes and valuables, preferably located close to the performance space.

Actors also need time for a variety of activities:

- **Warm-ups**—the vocal, physical, and mental exercises actors do to prepare for rehearsals and performances. The extent to which actors warm up and have developed a routine for doing so is usually a good indicator of their professionalism. Your responsibility is to provide sufficient time for this and a private, soundproof (or somewhat isolated) place in which to do it.
- **Memorization.** People's abilities to memorize vary greatly. You need to indicate when you expect actors to be "off book" (have the script memorized). Time in which to memorize should be included when you estimate your rate of pay. I recommend at least half an hour for memorization per minute of script for a monologue. In a show where an actor has a smaller role or two roles are equally shared, these hours could be reduced. It is not advisable to pay by the hour. Memorization time could vary by as much as twenty hours between performers.

- **Research**—the work you wish your actors to put into understanding content, context, character, background, and so on. Depending on the complexity and availability of the material (books, articles, recordings, videos), I recommend allowing at least half an hour per minute of script. If your script includes a bibliography and a list of research materials, you may wish to establish a time line by which you want the research accomplished. It is not advisable to pay by the hour; just as with memorization, people read at varying rates of speed.
- **Paperwork**—this could include script work, time sheets, memos, correspondence, and some degree of administrative paperwork.

WHAT YOU CAN EXPECT FROM PROFESSIONAL ACTORS
- Punctuality
- Early memorization of lines
- Thorough research
- A positive attitude toward the work

In all likelihood you will find that professional actors are resourceful and independent, possess a sense of humor and a variety of skills and interests.

A WORD (OR TWO) ON REFERENCES
CHECK THEM!

If your institution doesn't have a standard reference form for you to follow, devise one. Questions should include:

- Who am I talking to—a friend, a supervisor at a former job, a fellow worker?
- What did the working relationship consist of? Did they perform together? Was the applicant under the direction of the person giving the reference? Was one of them a teacher of the other?
- Would you repeat the experience?

Listen for nuances in the answers. "She's had a lot of experience since we last worked together" can mean: "You can risk hiring her if you want to, but I wouldn't touch her with a ten-foot pole." I once called an actor's former supervisor for a reference and was asked how I could put him in such an uncomfortable position. He had no desire to say anything negative about this person, he told me, speaking volumes by refusing to say anything at all. A potential employer once called one of SMM's presenters, given as a reference by an actress who had been fired. He was not asked a single question about his professional relationship to the person who had given him as a reference, or whether he was in a position to comment on her job performance. A glowing reference was given.

MUSEUMS' EXPERIENCES WITH PROFESSIONAL ACTORS

The Philadelphia Zoo Treehouse employed two to five staff performers who worked eight to thirty-five hours a week. It hired additional hourly staff, typically college students, during the summer months. Before the program closed in 2002, an internship program was operational, which included weekly workshops for performing and technical theatre majors, who had to audition for the program, and some of whom performed with the troupe. Treehouse performers who ran the Night Flight program were required to learn animal handling techniques, and all Treehouse members had to attend refresher courses. Treehouse staff also conducted presentation skills workshops for other departments, including training for docents and summer interns.

Explora hires paid professional actors from the Albuquerque area.

At the Museo de Historia Natural the theatre team is composed of secondary school teachers with experience in the country's highly regarded professional independent theatre. (Uruguay also has a state-supported national theatre.) These actors/teachers are paid at the same hourly rate they receive for other teaching assignments. Their areas of specialty include history, music, literature, and the plastic arts.

The Carnegie Museum of Natural History employs professional, paid performers. Like the Museo de Historia Natural, the Carnegie tried performers with a background in teaching. Unlike that of the Museo, the Carnegie's experience led Micheal List to conclude "that just because one can teach does not necessarily mean one can act."

The Witte Museum has no museum employees who "work solely on this program. All actors, directors, costumers, and playwrights are contracted by the museum and paid set fees. All but actors are paid one-time fees. Actors are contracted on a four- to six-month basis for weekly performances." Mellissa Marlowe, a performer and also coordinator of the program, works as "the coordinator of the outreach program on a contracted basis" and is paid a percentage of performance fees.

The Whitaker Center utilizes full- and part-time paid staff for their productions. "Two full-time and four part-time professional actors perform all of our presentations overseen by the Theatre and Outreach Manager. This is a full-time salaried position whose job description includes script development, staffing, and directing, as well as technical, marketing, and performance elements."

The Science Museum of Minnesota presently employs two full-time, salaried actors and hires part-time actors as needed.

COLOR-BLIND AND ETHNIC CASTING

Color-blind casting refers to assigning roles to actors regardless of their ethnicity. A father, mother, and children in a play, for example, could be of different skin color or ethnic backgrounds without the play making reference to it. Color-blind casting is sometimes used in commercial theatres, but it presents some singular difficulties for museums.

As part of the annual Theatre in Museums Workshop various ethnic performers and directors were invited to study museum theatre programs and the reasons for doing them, and to share their thoughts on color-blind casting. The conclusions they reached were as follows:

- For a performance in which history, race, or ethnicity is not central to the story, or in which the style of the performance is open and playful, there is no reason to consider race or ethnicity in casting. For example, in the play *Serendipity* three actors use characterization and puppets to explain how scientific discoveries have come about by chance. In a version in which an African American actress manipulated the puppet and provided the voice for a European American scientist no confusion was perceived on the part of the audience, and no misrepresentation resulted.
- For a performance in which historical accuracy or race and ethnic issues are central to the play, there is more to be lost than gained by casting an Asian American actress as Marie Curie or a white actor as George Washington Carver. These historical monologues are designed to present the person, his or her work, and the historical period in a realistic and accurate manner, and significant confusion could result if casting conventions were chal-

lenged. Many museumgoers may not have been exposed to the concept of color-blind casting, and watching a piece of theatre can be an unplanned event within their visit. Both these factors could contribute to very mixed feelings about their experience—feelings that could include confusion and racial tension, and could result in misinformation, involving the performer in explanations that have nothing to do with the goal of the presentation.

- The group agreed that, whenever possible, assuming an ethnicity not one's own was to be avoided. For example, if producing a play about recent Hmong settlers in the United States, every effort should be made to cast Hmong actors in those roles. The same would be true of a production featuring Native Americans. (Opinions vary on whether other Asian actors or Native Americans of different tribal affiliations should be cast in these roles.)

Exceptions to these guidelines occur as mentioned above, for puppeteers, and also when a storyteller or a character is talking *about* other ethnic groups. For example, a white storyteller may narrate an African story. She might, during the course of the story, bring out puppets, pictures, or props to aid her in telling the tale. The same would hold true of an African American performer telling a European or Asian tale. The storyteller is not pretending to be of a different ethnicity, but simply conveying the stories of other cultures. The portrayal of a historical character might include an episode in which a person of another ethnicity played a significant part. The actor might take on both roles during the delivery of the story.

Thoughtful consideration should be given to each particular situation. If you anticipate presenting a play in which any of these issues might be of concern, invite the opinion of people with experience of a similar kind within that ethnic group to aid you. Ethnic theatres are not uncommon, and they can be a source of advice and of leads to actors of that ethnicity.

An example of the care producers will take to assure ethnic authenticity is provided by the Smithsonian, where "scripts are subject to rigorous scrutiny. Because of the more ephemeral nature of 'programs,'" write Carolyn Rapkievian and Johanna Gorelick in their article "Beyond the Thanksgiving Myth," a theatrical production allows them "to look at an historical event from a different perspective, which in another context, could be seen as controversial."[3]

They describe their experience developing a piece that would

address the numerous questions from both teachers and students alike about
the relationship between the Indians and the pilgrims. In 1995, . . . Johanna selected two cultural interpreters, the Native guides who lead programs in the
Museum's galleries, who had theatre backgrounds to direct the production. Joe
Cross (Caddo/Potowatomi) and Donna Couteau (Sac/Fox) rewrote the script to
include music, dance, and audio-visual materials. In doing so, they researched
the Wampanoag thoroughly. They went to Plimoth Plantation where they met
with Nanapashmet, faithkeeper of the Wampanoag community. Part of their research was learning about the authentic ways that Wampanoag dressed in 1620,
what they ate and how their society was organized. It was also essential to them
that they understood 17th Century European society.[4]

■ ■ ■

In the twenty years I have been at the Science Museum of Minnesota it has been
my privilege to work with almost one hundred actors, some of them for a few
days, and many for several years. The experience has reduced me to tears many
times—particularly when I fired them. I inevitably felt that I had either done it
too soon or waited too long. Perhaps by the time I retire I will feel that I have finally got it right, but to me firing someone spells failure on both our parts. Since
I have little control over their part, I will share what I have learned on mine.

First, I have learned to trust my instincts. Whenever I felt that something
more was amiss than what was obvious (an actor was unprepared for rehearsals—always citing a reason; was often late—the person had incredibly
bad luck with buses or cars; experienced conflict with fellow workers—
accompanied usually with an inability to articulate what set the conflict off) I
found that my instincts were correct.

Second, I have learned to address the issue immediately, the first time it
happens, without waiting to see if it recurs. This does not have to be a hostile
confrontation, just a conversation that tells the actor that you have noticed the
behavior.

Third, I have learned that if it happens again, a verbal warning must be is-
sued and a note placed in my file of the date, time, place, and context of the
conversation.

Fourth, I have learned to issue a written warning at the third infraction.
This should state the fact that you have addressed the behavior verbally, and

outline clearly how you expect the behavior to change and by when. If lateness is an issue, your letter may state that you expect to see promptness for the next three weeks and lateness will be considered cause for termination.

Fifth, I have learned that the only evidence of change is change itself, not promises that change is coming ("when I move into a better apartment," "when I get over this cold," "when the situation with my girlfriend gets sorted out"). My most difficult experience with this was with a young actress who was a model of politeness and contrition, assuring me each time that this incident was the last. She was the first to acknowledge that she could not manage time and was always late, needing a lot of help with this issue—such as having to report her arrival to a floor manager, which kept her on track. She was also an excellent performer, and a master of denial. In spite of having received numerous warnings, when finally she was fired she was astonished and quite unable to understand why such a thing had happened to her.

If a situation doesn't improve immediately, it is highly unlikely that it ever will. I have discovered that I am much more at ease with my decisions if I have taken the time to document them. That way, when the time comes to take action I can revisit the behavior that brought us to this and dispel my concerns about being too hasty.

■ ■ ■

As an example of the versatility required of museum theatre performers, and of their willingness to use their diverse skills, I will conclude with some samples taken from the October 2003 monthly report submitted by Virginia Haggart, an actress at SMM. During that month, Virginia performed seventy-nine times in nine different shows, for approximately five thousand people. She also read *The Energy of Nature, Great Ideas in Physics, Seven Ideas that Shook the Universe,* and *The Biography of Medicine.* And from her two-page, single-spaced list of "Other tasks completed," I selected the following:

Glued diapers onto Indigo babies.

Taught a class on puppetry to fifty students.

Sewed dummy's armpit.

Put together three bamboo trees, added dental floss.

Painted Asi's hands and babies' heads.

Shopped for spider webs and mini pumpkins.

Fixed broken plastic skull.

Developed latex ghost trick.

NOTES

1. *Pittsburgh Post-Gazette,* quoted in Forbes, "Museum Theatre."

2. Bradley Zweig, "Profile: Theater at Please Touch Museum," *Museum Theatre Journal* 3 (1995).

3. Rapkievian and Gorelick, "Beyond the Thanksgiving Myth," *Museum Theatre Journal* 4 (Fall 1996). Rapkievian is Public Programs coordinator at the National Museum of the American Indian, and Gorelick is manager of the Cultural Interpreter Program.

4. Rapkievian and Gorelick, "Beyond."

7

Technical Requirements and Staff

An essential component of museum theatre is deciding on a location where performances will take place. Not all museums have an auditorium or stage available, and even those that do may make a conscious choice that performances will occur in gallery or exhibit spaces. In some cases, these spaces will have been designed with performances in mind, but more commonly, performances will be superimposed on existing designs. Either way, the following considerations are important:

- **Lighting.** Enough to ensure that the performers can be seen.
- **Sound.** Consideration needs to be given to sounds produced by the performance and sounds affecting it, such as noise levels from surrounding exhibits.
- **Space.** How much will be devoted to the performance and how much will be available for the audience members?
- **Traffic patterns** through and around the performance and audience spaces.

The extent of technical support museum theatre productions require can range from none to elaborate sets, props, lighting, and sound effects, and everything in between. All productions, however, require costuming. As Paul Short, one of the most talented costume designers ever to work in museum theatre, always said—"They may not need a set or props, they might get by without lighting or sound, but they *all* have to *wear* something!" In museum theatre, that is a safe assumption. We will therefore start with costuming as the one essential technical element.

COSTUME

If you are producing a piece of theatre set in the present and requiring no special items of clothing, you may choose not to pay someone to make sure that the performer wears what you consider appropriate. You will want to make it clear, however, that you, and not the performer, will be the one determining what that will be. Be warned, nonetheless, that actors, just like the rest of us, can be temperamental when it comes to appearance. They may be convinced that they look ghastly in certain colors, and quite fetching in pants with the crotch hanging between their knees.

Hair and shoes can also be an issue. Actors are used to being told what to wear onstage, and when left to their own devices may think nothing of gracing your stage looking as if they had never met a hairbrush or in shoes guaranteed to hamper their movement. When asked to wear something your institution may consider more appropriate, or to attend to their grooming, they invent imaginative reasons why they couldn't possibly comply. I thought I had heard them all until one lovely young woman explained that it was impossible for her to do anything with her hair during certain phases of the moon. At such times, she told me, her hair might start out in a neat bun, but was guaranteed to turn into a rat's nest by the end of the performance. Neither hairpins nor hair spray would tame her coiffure, which, if she was to be believed, was controlled entirely by the cosmos. While this is an extreme example, it is advisable to appoint someone to supervise costuming (which includes shoes, hats, and hair) even if ordinary street dress is called for.

Costumers come in several varieties: those who design only, those who build (sew) only, and those who do both. For most institutions the last is the best option. Designers who only design are typically expensive, and there is rarely a reason for using them. Exceptions might be difficult historical or ethnic costumes for which you need a specialist. Designers who only build will also not be very useful, unless you are asking them to copy from existing pictures. This has been true at art museums, for example, where a costumer is asked to reproduce the exact look in a painting.

Among the tasks a costumer performs are the following:

- Research—into the time period or style you want represented
- Design—drawing the costumes for your approval before buying the fabric or cutting it
- Shopping—for materials, sewing supplies, shoes, hats, gloves, and so on
- Drafting patterns. Some designers like to make their own patterns; others find it necessary to do so when making a costume for which a pattern is unavailable.
- Cutting
- Stitching
- Painting. Some designs require a fabric pattern that may be unavailable or highly specialized and has to be painted onto the fabric.
- Dying
- Fitting the costumes. Time must be allowed and a place found to fit the actor's costume.
- Acquiring wigs and accessories such as eyeglasses, jewelry, gloves, and purses

The Alchemist's Daughter *by Timothy Cope, performed by Steven Flamm and Kari Holmberg. Example of an exhibit area converted into a performance space. Photograph reprinted with permission of the Science Museum of Minnesota.*

How Do You Find a Costumer?

You find a costumer in the same places you looked for actors, directors, and writers—local theatres, and college and university theatre programs. You can let people know you're hiring by sending out a press release to these places, or by placing an ad in the employment section of your local paper, especially if it contains a theatre personnel section. Once again, be specific about your needs. For example:

> Costumer needed to design and build two 1870 women's day gowns. Please send letter of interest and resume by March 21 to _____. Previous experience required.

> Costumer needed to design and build a wearable and realistic Triceratops costume. Previous experience with body puppets a must.

What Do You Do When You Receive the Resumes in the Mail?

The theatre coordinator will review the resumes and select the three or four most qualified people. Before calling them in for an interview, the TC should be clear about deadlines and pay scale, and have a draft contract prepared to show the applicants. She should also know what questions she intends to ask during the interview and what she wants the applicant to bring. An experienced costumer will have a portfolio, which may include drawings, renderings, and photos. Renderings are usually in color and look like paintings. They may include fabric swatches. Drawings may also include swatches, but may be much less elaborate in style. Renderings often become the property of the theatre that commissioned them, so don't be surprised if your applicant has none. (They are quite costly.) Ask the applicant to bring the names and telephone numbers of at least two references. *Never fail to check them.* While actual costumes usually become the property of the theatre that commissioned them, it is advisable to ask the applicant to bring in something he has actually made, even if this is a contemporary piece of clothing.

Kari Holmberg, an experienced museum theatre costumer, recommends asking that the applicant bring in drawings or renderings and also photos of the final product, allowing you to assess whether or not the two resemble each other. Kari also pointed out that once hired, costumers should receive a copy of the script, and she provided the following fact to keep in mind: it takes about eight hours to make a tailored shirt, and about forty to build a three-piece suit. The costumer should also be informed of special needs that might not be obvious. Is a pocket a necessity? Will the actor be wearing a microphone that must be disguised by the costume or hidden under it? Will any fast changes out of one costume and into another be required?

It is important that the costumer meet with the director of the show. At this time, the director will make clear her ideas for the costumes.

The Interview

Focus on experience. When interviewing a designer about historical costuming, for example, it is key to inquire how the costume will be built from the skin out. Undergarments and foundation garments are essential to the design and look of any period costume, and a costumer who does not appear to be aware of this should not be considered for such a project.

It is also important to establish where the work will take place. Occasionally, when applying to an institution, costumers will assume that you have a sewing room, or at least an area set aside for the work of cutting and stitching. Some may assume you will also provide all the necessary equipment. It is important to include this discussion in your interview. Does the applicant have a place to perform the work, and the equipment needed to perform it? How will he transport the items? Will you be charged if a cab or car rental is required? Will you pay for mileage if the costumer uses his own car?

What Does a Costumer Get Paid?

Once more, local research is best. Find out what costumers are being paid at both professional and community theatres, determine how those pay scales fall within your institution's pay scale and budget, and decide accordingly. It is typical to pay half the fee up front and half on satisfactory completion. This arrangement should be laid out in the contract.

It is important to discuss with the costumer payment for materials.

- Does your institution have an account at a fabric store, a shoe store, or other store that you expect the costumer to use?
- Will you advance money for materials? If so, what are your expectations regarding receipts?

- Is the costumer willing to spend his own money and be reimbursed by you? If so, the contract should state how much the costumer is entitled to spend and the time limit within which reimbursement can be expected.

Scheduling

Plans need to be made for presenting the sketches to the people responsible for approving them, fittings, and a photo shoot (optional).

The Contract

The contract should include the following:

- Deadlines. When is the dress rehearsal? When is the first performance? When do you want the costumes finished?
- Maintenance information. Will the costumer be responsible for ongoing maintenance (cleaning, ironing, repairs) or be called in only for major damages or refitting for a new performer?
- Is the costumer required to attend the dress rehearsal or any of the performances?

Maintenance and Cleaning

Included in your contract with the costumer will be a time line detailing when the costumer's responsibilities to you end. This could be at the time of handing over the costumes or at the end of the run. What is your plan for repairs, replacements, and upkeep, including cleaning? If you want the costumer to assume responsibility for any of these tasks, a schedule and fees need to be determined. If the actors are going to be responsible for any part of the maintenance (stitching up a hem, sewing on a button) or for the cleaning, then the materials for repairs need to be provided (needles, matching thread, etc.), and washing instructions included with the costumes.

In some areas, dry cleaning services pick up and deliver.

PROP AND SET DESIGNER

In traditional theatre, the jobs of designing sets and props are not always combined. A prop is a moveable item brought in, taken out, or used by the performers. A set is a painted backdrop, staircase, or other unit moved, if at all, only during changes of scene, and furniture. In museum theatre, it would be unusual to hire separately for these functions.

Some props are easily obtainable, some are not. Museum theatre productions frequently call for the use of reproductions of period props such as pots, utensils, or tools, cultural items of clothing or daily use, weapons, and crafts. Some element of the set or a particular prop may require specialized expertise, in which case the set designer might chose to hire that piece out. Examples could be the reproduction of a painting or some other work of art, a mechanical device, or some highly specialized piece of machinery.

Many museum theatre productions are performed without a set, using exhibits as backdrops, or utilizing only props. Set pieces can range from elaborate to simple. It all depends on locale, budget, and staff.

Performances may take place in the following places:

- Exhibit areas, utilizing set pieces that are not a permanent part of the exhibit, for instance, a backdrop that will be brought in and taken out again when the show is over
- Exhibit areas designed for performance. These areas may include a small stage, lighting, and seating. Some may be so well integrated into the exhibit that they are exhibits in and of themselves. An example of this was found in the touring Gold Exhibit, in which an alchemist's shop, complete in its own right, included a mannequin of an alchemist surrounded by all his equipment. At the time of the performance, the mannequin and some portable items were removed, leaving the floor clear for a performance. Areas such as these can be designed with storage and with fixtures that allow for change, such as places on which to hang different backdrops, or windows that can be revealed or disguised.
- A theatre. In these areas, designed to accommodate sets, we may find actual flats (a covered framework), puppet stages, or other set elements.
- At times, big artifacts on display will serve as sets for museum theatre productions. At the Canadian Museum of Civilization, for example, actors performed on a train.

The following questions are important to consider when commissioning and designing a set:

- Who will set it up for each performance?
- Who will take it down after the performance?

- How much and what kind of equipment is needed to install and remove the set?
- Who will repair and maintain it?

In typical museum theatre situations, a crew is not employed, and actors are asked to handle these technical elements. It is therefore important to make them as light, portable, and easy to handle as possible. This needs to be conveyed clearly at the interview and included in the contract at the time of hiring a designer. Like costumers, set designers sometimes design without building. I recommend combining the two, for the same reasons outlined in the section on costuming.

How Do You Find a Set Designer?

Follow the guidelines provided for costumers. The sample ads below can be used as guides.

Wanted, set designer and builder for small, lightweight, portable puppet stage.

Wanted, set designer and builder for nineteenth-century sod house. Must provide own work space and transportation.

Once more, the theatre coordinator will review the resumes, select two or three candidates, and ask them to come in for an interview. They will be asked to bring their portfolios, which will include examples of their work in the form of photographs, plans, and drawings. I find it extremely helpful for designers to provide three-dimensional mock-ups, or small models of a set they have designed. If the designers have these and they are easily transportable, you may ask to see one at the interview.

Preparing for the Interview

Whether you are hiring for a specific project or for a series of shows, the designer is likely to ask for as much information as you can provide. This information will include the following:

- Budget
- Style of the production, for instance: "The set and furnishings must accurately reflect an upper-class Philadelphia home in 1850."

- Special needs, for instance: "Actors must be able to safely stand on a platform six feet above the stage."
- Time line

Maintenance and Repairs

Just as with the costumes, it is a good idea to have thought through your expectations regarding who will be maintaining the set and props and repairing them when necessary. If the designer is not a museum employee, she may assume that the job is completed upon delivery and that nothing further is expected. You may want to build into the contract a maintenance clause for the time the play is running.

It is also important to consider what you intend to do with the set and the props when the play is finished. Do you intend to keep and store them? Give them away? If storage is an option, then dimensions need to be taken into account, as does transportation if the storage space is off site.

Pay

The same method should be employed here as is by now familiar to you—check around and see what others are paying and decide on a fee that is fair to the designer and to you. Also, see the recommendations regarding the purchase of costuming materials. The same guidelines apply to set and prop designers. I recommend paying not by the hour, but by the job.

The Contract

The contract should include the following:

- Deadlines
- Pay schedule. It is typical to pay half the money at the beginning of the project and the second half upon satisfactory completion. The same considerations regarding paying for materials need to be taken into account for props and set as for costumes.
- Clear listing of all expectations and responsibilities in as much detail as you can provide, for example: "Contractor will deliver a platform five by six feet wide and six feet tall, constructed to hold four actors safely. Platform must fit through all elevator and exhibit entrance doors."
- A copy of the script should be provided.

Budget Considerations

If you have a fixed budget for set and prop materials for your show, for example $500, I recommend that you tell the designer that you have $400. Cost overruns are commonplace.

Questions the Designer Will Ask

- What is the budget?
- Where will the performance take place? (The designer will study sight lines and audience placement.)
- What are the maximum conceivable stresses to be placed on the set? How many people will use it at a time?
- Who will maintain the set and props?
- How will change be dealt with? (Time and money should be allocated and changes expected.)
- Who does the designer report to?
- Who does the designer go to when she has a question?
- Will anyone other than the theatre coordinator, director, or producer have a say in the design?
- Will the designer build the set on site? If not, will you pay for transportation?

Questions the Designer May Not Know to Ask about Museum Theatre

- Will the audience be coming and going?
- Will there be audience participation in the show? Does this entail someone coming up on stage, using a prop? Is audience and/or performer safety a concern?
- Will the set remain up between performances or be taken down? If it will be taken down, who will do this? How many people? How much time is allotted for this task? Where will the set be stored and who will have access to it? What obstructions or constrictions might there be between the performance and the storage area?
- How long will the set and props be in use? Does the show run for a week or a year? (This and the previous questions will affect the choice of materials and the construction.)

EXAMPLES FROM THE PARTICIPATING INSTITUTIONS

Explora uses paid prop and set builders, and video and lighting specialists from local theatres; while at the Museo de Historia Natural the theatre team does all of its own technical work; and at the Carnegie the program specialist takes care of all the props, sets, and costumes. At the Whitaker Center sound, lighting, and props are handled in-house. "These," Buss says, "make great projects for actors. . . . Set design and building is often done by a scene designer we hire from the community. . . . Costumes are often purchased, but we have hired costume designers in the past."

Evaluations and Visitor Perspective Findings

Two things I learnd from your speech are, that if you are a womon you can do just what men do just the same as them. Also that bugs are a big part of our lives and they are just like us exept for entenis, and more legs.

—*Katelyn Price, fourth-grade student, after seeing a performance of* Anna and the Insects *at the SMM*

As a technique, theatre has proven effective and appealing, as evidenced by the fact that in one form or another, it has been a part of every culture and society for centuries. Museums, however, are frequently asked to compare theatre to other forms of interpretation, or to justify its effectiveness as an interpretive, educational technique.

Evaluating the effectiveness of museum theatre programs is as challenging as evaluating any other educational program, largely because the term *education* covers a wide spectrum of outcomes. Most museums would consider a museum visit successful from an educational standpoint if the visitor

- acquires measurable new knowledge (i.e., facts);
- gains a new or different perspective (e.g., cultural, historic, scientific, or artistic);
- engages in an inquiry or discussion regarding an exhibit or exhibit component; or
- applies knowledge gained from the visit to present or future life choices.

George E. Hein and Mary Alexander tell us that

one of the marvels of museums is that the brief encounters visitors have with
exhibitions do appear to lead to learning, do result in some change in the visitor that is often remembered with pleasure, and can influence future behavior.
Personal stories of the power of museum visits to transform lives have frequently been reported. . . . But what we know about the nature of that learning
is still elusive and incomplete. The ephemeral nature of most museum visits,
typically of short duration and relatively infrequent, clearly affects research evidence. . . . A common finding from experimental design studies that separate
cognitive and affective domains is that museum visits—to a science museum
(Flaxner and Borun 1984) or history museum (Boggs 1977)—result in more
change in affect than in cognition. . . . Others who view the museum experience
as a holistic event (Silverman 1995) report that museum visits result in changes
that can be described as learning, such as identifying one's own experience with
that of the people depicted in a history exhibition, relating science exhibitions
to familiar phenomena, or being inspired to generate visual images by visiting
an art museum. . . . How visitors make meaning from museums is greatly influenced by their previous knowledge, attitudes, and interests. This complex inter-
play between what visitors bring with them and what they take away ensures
that museum visits are multifaceted, highly personal experiences with the potential for significant learning. . . . The short and long-term effects of these mul-
tilayered interactions cannot be overestimated. And the learning they
stimulate—learning of many kinds, appealing to multiple styles and purposes—
can be had in this depth and variety literally nowhere else.[1]

The same holds true for the museum theatre experience.

As reported in the November 1998 edition of *Aviso*, the National Endowment for the Arts conducted a survey in 1997 regarding public participation in
the arts. Of the seven arts activities listed (museums, jazz and classical concerts,
opera, musicals, plays, and ballet), museums were the most popular. Sixty-eight
million people are estimated to attend museums at least once a year.[2]

In the winter edition of the *Arts Board News* the Minnesota State Arts
Board reported on a study conducted by the Performing Arts Research Coali-
tion. The research was funded by the Pew Charitable Trusts and focused on
"the value placed on the performing arts by attenders and nonattenders." The
research revealed that "more Americans surveyed attended a professional per-

forming arts event than attended a professional sporting event," and that "a very high value" was placed

> on the role of the arts in their lives in terms of enjoyment, their understanding of themselves and other cultures, creativity, and connection to their communities. . . . They believe strongly that the arts improve the quality of life and are a source of community pride, promote understanding of other people and different ways of life, and help preserve and share cultural heritage. Above all, they believe that the arts contribute to the education of children. Especially noteworthy is the fact that a majority of nonattenders share similar views about the education and development of children and that this view is held regardless of education, income, age, presence of children at home, or frequency of attendance.[3]

In 1990, the Baltimore City Life Museums conducted a study comparing theatre and exhibits. More than three hundred visitors were surveyed, and, as reported by Serkownek, between 77 and 96 percent of them found theatre to be better than exhibits at "presenting information in a meaningful and enjoyable manner," imparting "knowledge about nineteenth-century Maryland history," and allowing "self-exploration of historical information."[4]

In 1983, the Smithsonian's National Museum of American History compared 160 visitors' reactions to experiencing the Virginia Parlor exhibit only (sixty-five respondents) and the play (ninety-five respondents) performed in the parlor. Seventy-two percent of the visitors who visited the parlor and saw the play made a connection between life in the 1700s and today. By contrast, only 58 percent of those who only experienced the parlor made that connection. The ninety-five respondents who saw the play agreed that "the drama was significantly more active and involving than the traditional presentation of the period room."

In his article "Museum Theatre and Evaluation: An Overview of What We Know," Dale Jones reports that

> there is some growing evidence that visitors do, in fact, learn from their museum theatre experience. In an evaluation at the Museum of Science, Boston, authors Baum and Hughes report giving pre- and post-tests to a random sample of visitors: "Visitors were given three multiple-choice questions about Chico's (Chico Mendes') biography, extractive reserves, and cattle ranching. Of the post-test group, 80% chose the correct answer to the question about Chico

Mendes, compared to 27% of the pre-test group. For the question about extractive reserves, 98% of the post-test group defined this concept accurately, compared to 35% of the pre-test group." In 1999 I conducted an evaluation of an exhibition and museum theatre performance at the Hershey Museum and decided to compare the visitors who had seen the performance and exhibition versus those who had seen only the exhibition. The results were startling! When asked what they could remember about one of the three main themes of the exhibition, 94% of visitors who saw the performance could recall information, while only 58% of visitors who saw just the exhibition could recall some fact. In another instance only 33% of those seeing only the exhibition recalled information, while 69% of those seeing the performance could recall relevant information.[5]

Catherine Vincent of the National Aquarium at Baltimore wrote of the aquarium's evaluation of outreach programs for fourth-grade students,

Teachers have noted in their evaluation how differently their students behave. Students who regularly have problems focusing, are the class clown, or are generally uninterested were highly engaged and hooked into the labs. Students who previously disdained science were up to their elbows in mud and remain highly interested in the Chesapeake Bay. . . . Anecdotal stories and direct observations indicate that the theatre experience, based on a first person, real life situation does facilitate a higher level of engagement in the lab. . . . When only the lab was presented to students, the difference in the behavior and attitude between these student groups and those who had seen the play was striking. Lab-only students went through the lab stations completing the tasks. . . . However, these students tended to be less engaged in the lab activities. They spent less time at each station, wandered off teasing each other and squirting one another with water. . . . This group had the facts, but lacked the attitudinal shift and the emotional connection that leads to internalizing information and making changes in the real world. . . . The overwhelming success of this program has led to renewed funding [from the Chesapeake Bay Trust].[6]

In 1988, D. Stuart Miller, currently the executive director of the Sautee Nacoochee Center, wrote his master's thesis on "The Effect of Interpretive Theatre on Children in the Museum Setting." A significant percentage of his research was conducted at the SMM, where he observed the actions of children between the ages of seven and twelve in the Anthropology Hall over a three-week period. Performances took place in the area of the hall where the Egyptian mummy was displayed. Above the performance area there was a boardwalk that allowed Miller to observe without being observed.

My study ... found that a performance typically attracted between one-half and three-quarters of all individuals within the hall at the time the performance began. The attraction to the performance occurred even if that exhibit was in a remote corner of the hall. The effect was akin to placing a magnet in the vicinity of scattered paper clips. . . . In addition to attracting visitors to an area of the museum, interpretive theatre performances hold them there for extended periods. . . . The average amount of time spent within the exhibition area when theatre was not employed was one minute twenty-seven seconds when no docent was on duty in the exhibit area, and one minute forty-five seconds when a docent was present. Factoring in attendance to the performance within the exhibit area, children spent an average of eighteen minutes five seconds within the exhibition space. Results from this study concluded, that theatre not only attracted visitors to an exhibit area, but that it also held visitors in an exhibit area. . . . Children who observed the *Akh* presentation stayed in the exhibit area for an average of 18:05. Children who viewed only the Egypt exhibit without the interpretive theatre piece spent 1:27 investigating the exhibit.

In 1989, SMM evaluated the fifteen plays running in the museum at the time. The evaluation was conducted over three months by means of interviews. Audiences leaving performances were asked to answer a series of quite general questions designed to tell evaluators whether they felt that theatre had added to their visit, and some specific ones focusing on understanding and retention of content. The questions about content were based on the goals of the piece. For example, one of the goals for the play on Ka, one of the spirits of the Egyptian mummy, was to explain "the religious beliefs behind the process of mummification."

The study revealed that audiences were virtually unanimous in their agreement that theatre had enhanced their visit to the museum. In describing what they had derived from the performances, 97 percent of the 414 adults interviewed used language almost identical to the language contained in the program goals.

Carol Lynn Duganne, education associate for classroom services at the Witte Museum in San Antonio, Texas, writes in the spring 1995 issue of the *Journal* that "written evaluations, in addition to observations, measured the impact of the museum's gallery theater performances. Comments were rewarding. 'The play was the best part'; 'My children, ages 9, 6, and 3 were enthralled'; 'It was a wonderful learning experience'; and 'emotionally moving. I'll never forget it.'"[7]

Explora conducted a two-year evaluation of its theatre programs from 1999 to 2001, to assess whether theatre performances supported the institution's mission to create "opportunities for inspirational discovery and the joy of lifelong learning through interactive experiences in science, technology, and art." It concluded that

> each performance provided an opportunity for the audience to become actively engaged in examining ideas, attitudes, and values in a highly personalized way as they learned. The performances promoted true learning through emotional involvement, critical thinking, and the opportunity for participants to construct their own meaning.

One of the questions the evaluator asked was "Did the performance enhance visitor museum experiences?" Explora concluded that "Ninety-one percent of those who completed surveys expressed the opinion that performances like the ones they viewed add a lot to museums."

The Museo de Historia Natural has devoted as much time to evaluating the results of its efforts as it has to developing the performances, with one of the teachers on the theatre team assuming this task as an integral part of her work assignment for the museum. She conducted an evaluation in which it was determined that people who attend the performances are significantly more engaged and interested during subsequent tours than those who do not.

Detailed questionnaires were also given to students and to teachers who attended the performances. Results determined that 97 percent of the students had learned something new and 74 percent had had their point of view altered. Follow-up questions were designed to elicit the veracity of these perceptions, and confirmed them. Teachers also indicated that they had learned from the performances, and that the most satisfying element for them was the degree to which their students enjoyed themselves.

The Minnesota Historical Society evaluated its interpretive programming in 1995, 1997, and 2000. The 1995 study was a general evaluation of interpretive programming seeking to measure attraction and holding power of interpretive programs, the level of interaction, and the communicative (cognitive impact goals) and connecting (visitor relates personal past to "museum" history) impact. One hundred and seventy-eight brief, structured interviews were conducted immediately after participation in the program.

This phase of the study concluded that "49 percent of adults and 59 percent of children stopped and participated in stage shows when offered. . . . Ninety-five percent of visitors who participated in a program felt that it made their visit to the History Center more enjoyable." The reasons fell into five basic themes:

1. Program made history personal, live, or real
2. Program engaged visitor more than other exhibit components
3. Program increased visitor learning
4. Social experience enhanced visit
5. Program was entertaining

The second phase, in 1997, involved the "first use of formal museum theatre (tightly scripted, multiple characters in a show)." Adults were interviewed and children invited to draw "a picture about what they just saw and then describe their picture." This study concluded that performances were an extremely effective means of engaging visitors in difficult topics related to family life. Benefits of performances listed by visitors fell into several categories:

- Made history come alive
- Were more engaging that other aspects of the exhibits
- Enhanced learning
- Added to visitor enjoyment
- Combined well with the exhibit experience

It was clear from the children's drawings and descriptions that they had understood "the relationships between the characters and the emotions the characters were experiencing."

The third phase of the study was designed to "determine if goals for cognitive and affective learning were met, and to assess overall visitor satisfaction with plays." Visitors were randomly selected as they left the performance and asked to fill out a survey. One hundred percent of them agreed to do so. This study reached the following conclusions:

- Visitors rated all plays as highly educational and interesting.
- Eighty-five percent of participants attributed some impact on their understanding of the exhibit to the play.
- Twenty-two percent said they "learned another perspective" from the play.
- Visitors were less surprised by what they learned in the plays than they were by the plays themselves. Production details, such as the quality of the acting and authenticity of characters, costumes, and so on, were listed by over half of the participants as something that surprised them about the play.
- The four different plays elicited a mixture of cognitive and affective responses from visitors.
- Visitors took away the intended messages of each play.

Hans Joachim Klein of Karlsruhe University in Germany, a specialist in visitor research and evaluation, conducted a study on a temporary exhibition—100 Years of Radio Waves—at the university and on its closely integrated theatre performance. The focus of the exhibition was Heinrich Hertz, who discovered and proved the existence and properties of waves, paving the way for the invention of the wireless telegraph, radio, and television.

Reactions to the inclusion of theatre in the exhibition "ran the entire spectrum: from friendly acceptance to an exuberant enthusiasm," Klein reported. Comments included: "It was history that one could really relate to, and for those who didn't know much about the subject beforehand, the play provided a visual representation of the concepts which will be remembered longer than a lot of exhibit text and artifacts." "As a physicist, I found the play very enjoyable, the use of the language of the time along with manners, showed another dimension of the times."

Professor Klein also discovered that

even if visitors did not understand completely the meaning of complex connections, they got an idea of "how it could be approximately." Many of them were unable or unwilling to follow these first steps of reflection when the same context was presented to them in the form of written texts. Last, but not least, the content of the play provoked the visitor to go back into the exhibition for a second time. Visitors were frequently observed talking about the artifacts and accompanying documents on display. They noted that they were looking at the objects with "new eyes" now that they "understood what they were seeing."[8]

EVALUATING YOUR THEATRE PROGRAM

The most challenging part of conducting effective evaluation is also the most basic—determining what it is you want to evaluate and for what purpose. First, return to the statement you made in reply to the question "Why do you want to use theatre?" If the purpose of your evaluation is to determine whether or not you are fulfilling your stated mission, the questions you will address to your visitors will be clear. If you want to evaluate a particular presentation, examine what triggered this desire for evaluation. Was it that evaluations are trendy, and since everyone else is doing one surely you must follow suit? Or is there something you really need or want to know about how audiences are responding to your program? Such information can include understanding whether the program is meeting its goals; estimating whether audiences perceive the program as adding value to their visit; and determining the number of visitors who participate in the program and their level of participation.

Evaluation can take the form of oral interviews, written questionnaires, and observation of visitor behavior and reactions. Not to be discounted are the performers' observations of visitor reactions and the kinds of questions and comments visitors have for them.

The way information will be used often determines how it is collected. There are three primary uses for evaluations. The first is internal, a means for assessing the effectiveness of the program and its technique. An example of this is the audience count actors keep for each SMM performance. The total number of people who see the programs averages 125,000 per year, between 10 and 15 percent of visitors. Interpreting these numbers became of vital importance during a period of budget cuts. Local commercial theatres were asked to share their attendance numbers, revealing that 125,000 exceeded the attendance at most of them, and was rivaled only by the Guthrie Theatre and the Chanhassen Dinner Theatre complex. The delivery of programs at SMM was achieved for a fraction of the cost and personnel utilized in commercial theatres. Even keeping in mind that museum theatre programs are considerably shorter and far less sophisticated in terms of technical support, 125,000 people represented an impressive figure.

The second use of evaluation is for reporting to state agencies, sponsors, or partners. The third is for fund-raising. Facts and figures are important. Equally so are anecdotes that support the impact of a program. Recently, a young woman approached a performer who was cleaning up after a show and introduced herself. She had seen that same show when she was in grade school and it had so sparked her interest in science that she had participated in and won several competitions with her science projects. She was also contemplating a science career. Often, it is the anecdotes that save the day, and encouraging actors and presenters to note and collect them is vital.

NOTES

1. Hein and Alexander, *Museums: Places of Learning* (Washington, DC: American Association of Museums, 1998).

2. American Association of Museums, *Aviso* (November 1998).

3. *The Arts Board News*, "The Value of the Performing Arts" (Winter 2004).

4. Serkownek, "Museum Theatre."

5. Jones, "Museum Theatre and Evaluation: An Overview of What We Know," *Insights* (Summer 2000).

6. Vincent, "Bay on the Road: The Traveling Theatre Science Program of the National Aquarium of Baltimore," *Museum Theatre Journal* 5 (Fall 1997).

7. Duganne, "Profile: Witte Museum," *Museum Theatre Journal* 3 (1995).

8. Klein, "Exhibit Theater as an Interpretive Tool" (unpublished paper).

9

Selling the Idea

Persuading educators that theatre will support their goals and add interesting dimensions to interpretive programs typically poses less difficulty than persuading boards of directors, funders, and presidents to provide the necessary resources. Among the practical objections raised by the latter are justifying the cost of the program, devoting spaces to theatre needs, and hiring specialized personnel. Among the philosophical issues are compatibility of goals and purpose (between the institution and theatrical programming) and concerns about entertainment and education. We have already looked at the practical questions in chapters 4 through 6, and at the use of evaluation to demonstrate the value of theatre programs in chapter 8. The focus here will be on philosophical issues and justifying the use of theatre as an educational technique.

At the Children's Museum of Indianapolis, Larry Gard reported in 1994 that both staff and volunteers learned "that entertainment is an essential element in the life and well-being of our institution, for entertainment not only serves education—it brings a lot of people through the door!"[1] As far back as 1964, Gard reminds us, Henry D. Brown wrote, "Museum personnel must recognize that visitors are under no obligation or requirement to render studious attention to museum exhibits, nor even to enter your building. Consequently, it is expedient to intrigue before you instruct!"[2] In his "Entertainment in Education: A Justification," Gard writes, "The idea of merging entertainment with education has raised more institutional eyebrows than any of us would care to acknowledge. To some educators, entertainment smacks of the frivolous and bizarre."[3]

Gard expresses concern that administrators might consider entertainment a trivial pursuit.

> For certain administrators, the conflict has mistakenly placed Mission versus Market. In some cases it has erroneously positioned programmers versus curators and exhibit designers. Moreover, entertainment can be expensive—especially in the form of quality gallery theatre. Knowing the great value of utilizing live theatre as an interpretive device, many of us have fought time and again to meet that incessant fiscal command: "Justify! Justify! Justify!" The ensuing argument has pitted museum theatre professionals against those monstrous three B's of the museum world: Board, Budget and Bureaucracy. Unfortunately, the result has been the downfall of many new and innovative museum theatre programs. Unfortunately, people often limit their idea of entertainment by isolating experiences that are simply fun, amusing or pleasant, and not necessarily as experiences that spark interest, desire or curiosity. . . . Entertainment such as gallery theatre creates a "conversation" of sorts between a visitor and an exhibit. In a direct sense, the entertaining element intrigues the visitor and thus creates an impetus to be even more involved. Indirectly, it creates a temptation to learn. It is a palatable recipe of both entertaining and educational components—a give-and-take swirl of feeling and information—blending an intriguing encounter with an educationally sound experience.

Dr. Cindi Gonzales, an education specialist at the University of Texas Institute of Culture in San Antonio, also encountered concern on the issue of entertainment and education, and was asked to justify the cost of her theatre program. She began by consulting her file of articles on the effectiveness of museum theatre as a teaching tool, but it was the telephone calls from schools asking for theatre programs that tipped the balance in her favor. "The power of our gallery theatre was best summed up by one postperformance interviewee—'The play touches my heart, and I felt connected to the writer who brought this play to us! I enjoyed learning more about my heritage in this performance.'" The success of the program brought administrative and budget support, and museum theatre acquired "a powerful voice . . . that speaks with a Texas drawl."[4]

Museums that utilize outreach programs as a means of serving audiences unable to visit their site often select theatre as a vehicle. An unusual example of an outreach performance took place on the Allegheny River. "In 1995," Serkownek reports,

> the Venango Museum of Art, Science, and Industry sponsored a traveling theater outreach program to accompany a raft trip down the Allegheny River from Warren, Pennsylvania, to Pittsburgh on a reproduction nineteenth-century packet boat. The boat's crew tied up in a new community each evening and performed a play, *Oil on the Brain*, which highlighted the region's oil history.

A land-based example of successful outreach is at the Pittsburgh Children's Museum, where "performances attract good publicity. . . . The shared, focused attention of a performance offers visitors a striking counterpoint to the exuberantly free-form exploration taking place in the rest of the museum."[5] The Pittsburgh Children's Museum began with in-house performances and, after obtaining a grant for this purpose, toured its programs to schools, discovering that outreach was often an introduction to the museum and what it had to offer to schools. "Field trips and requests for more outreach programs frequently followed a performance. Moreover, assembly programs successfully played to kindergarten through sixth-grade audiences, thereby breaking down a misconception that the museum is for preschool and primary-grade children only." The Pittsburgh Children's Museum found that their touring theatre show generated income for the museum, with 40 percent of the profit from the booking fees returned to the museum. The museum has reached more than eighty thousand children each year in their own schools. Lois Winslow, the museum's education and outreach coordinator, has found that

> the theatre process acts as a dynamic teacher of teachers as it demonstrates how creative, interactive approaches to learning can engage children effectively. . . . Theatre has become the educational mainstay of our extremely successful outreach program. . . . All of our productions tie closely into the elementary and middle school curriculum or come suggested by educators as subjects of concern that ought to be addressed for children. Our plays cover such diverse themes as health, environmental responsibility, the Pittsburgh steel industry heritage, story building skills, goal setting, good choices, alternatives to TV viewing, safety, science, career selection and gender bias.[6]

Winslow adds that theatre techniques at her institution are also used "to improve the skills of our floor staff." Theatre exercises are planned to be a part of everyday preparations and staff training. "Warm-up and voice exercises, voice projection and body posture—all theatre techniques—can make for more effective communication with museum visitors." Theatre Program staff offer presenter training sessions for other staff members, creative drama lesson plans for gallery application, and storytelling sessions in the galleries.

Institutions frequently list ways of promoting their activities to new or underserved audiences among their goals, something theatre can also support. The Minnesota Children's Museum came up with an innovative way of promoting the work of the museum and also of obtaining ideas for new plays from children who might not yet have visited the museum. John Stout initiated an annual short story contest cosponsored by the *St. Paul Pioneer Press.* In this case, the writers were all children themselves. The winners had their stories published in the newspaper, and one was selected for dramatization. In 1993 the newspaper received six thousand entries.

Marlowe of the Witte believes that museum theatre has helped "to create interest in objects on exhibit that might otherwise be overlooked," and Carol Lynn Duganne, education associate for Classroom Services, writes,

> Before the introduction of gallery theatre, I observed visitors lingered about 1 or 2 minutes at an exhibit featuring small detailed 19th century oil paintings of a south Texas locale. After our first gallery theatre performance, the audience, en masse, got up and headed for the paintings. They looked closely, read labels, talked to each other and enthusiastically spent time in an exhibit area where before they had hurriedly passed through. Even the administration staff, who had to walk by the performance area on the way to their offices, would stop and watch. Each performance added more proof that gallery theater could attract, hold, and educate in ways the paintings themselves could not.[7]

Marlowe adds that theatre has also helped "to transform uninviting and cold spaces into warm and inviting ones." The Witte's play *Encounter at Panther Cave* was written to support the exhibit Ancient Texans, Life along the Lower Pecos. It is

> the story of a modern-day archaeologist meeting the spirit of an ancient shaman on the site of ancient cave paintings. When performing the play, the ac-

tors employ several props, some new camping equipment, and some replicas of the artifacts found in the exhibit, and a large flat painted with recreations of the paintings found in the actual Panther Cave in the Lower Pecos region of Texas. It has been my experience that the audience members (especially children) take a great interest in these props and have many questions about them. . . . If they have already seen the exhibit, the use of replicas helps to create an understanding of how the objects were actually used and for what purposes. . . . It also helps to support understanding of a culture with no written language, a concept sometimes not considered by school children.

Juliet Breckenridge, visitor programs specialist at the Monterey Bay Aquarium, reports that the aquarium finds theatre valuable for presenting information about animals that cannot be brought out for the public and included in demonstrations and shows. Of the moment when she discovered the power of the technique, she says,

Watching a performance of *The Road from Ban Vinai*[8] . . . I understood the true power of theatre. . . . It is a first-person story about the son of a Vietnam veteran who describes his experiences while visiting a Hmong refugee camp in Thailand. . . . The day before I had walked through this same space and glanced past the signage and displays with no interest. Now, watching the performance, this exhibit, the cultural dress, the artifacts in the museum's collection, the whole space, suddenly became personally interesting. After watching the piece I felt compelled to read the signs and explore the Hmong culture further. Theatre transformed me from a passive observer into an active participant. . . . This is what theatre can do, and do so well if done right. . . . Theatre can reach the heart. Once the heart is involved, teaching the facts, history, and science is a breeze.[9]

Science Museum of Virginia dramaturge Twyla Kitt says that theatre programs support and enhance her museum's mission, established by an act of the state legislature in 1970 "to stimulate an interest in, and increase the understanding of, science and technology for all people." The Science Museum of Virginia is

in the business of getting nonscientists to do science with their hands, heads, and senses. Our core ideology is to make people think by providing lively, fun, and engaging experiences. Our team innately values self-discovery, learning, creativity, innovation, honesty, and integrity. There is an energy created between live actors and an audience that is unique, and this energy invites the audience to enter into the experience that unfolds onstage. The emotional connection created during this experience provides unparalleled opportunities for introducing science concepts.

The museum has many interactive exhibits and offers a wide scope of educational programs, but "it is the theatre program . . . that attracts the broadest cross section of the public, including those who may not be predisposed to investigate science."

Dornfest adds, "Plays provide compasses for further emotional and intellectual journeys, establishing a shared starting place and illuminating some of the pathways for exploration."

Charged with increasing attendance, helping people value the objects displayed in the museum, and raising ecological awareness, Lucía Todone of the Museo de Historia Natural discovered in museum theatre a "motivator, a link between art and science," and—interestingly—"a revealer of vocations." She believes that its greatest strength is working with the senses. Among the events that motivated her to begin exploring this technique was the use of radio soap operas in Colombia, where peasants were in the habit of clear cutting land by burning. To discourage a practice resulting in environmental harm, the government embarked on an educational campaign including the use of books and the distribution of flyers from airplanes. The clear cutting continued—until the government decided to write a soap opera in which the main character changed his behavior under the good influence of his girlfriend.

Sheehy of the Weisman believes that "theatre also helps us to connect to broader audiences, bringing in people from the theatre, dance, and spoken word communities, both artists and their followers. I have to say, too, from a staff perspective, that our theatre program keeps us vital."

Edith Serkownek tells us that

> the idea that theater may serve as an important tool for recreating what is known as the object's original context is central to the mission statement of the Canadian Museum of Civilization's theater program. The program's mission "is to present interpretive theatre in order to contextualize objects and information intellectually, emotionally, socially, politically, spiritually and aesthetically."

Serkownek adds that museums use theatre both "to contextualize and to personalize, with actors mediating between the visitor and the object by giving the object emotional as well as factual content."

Not to be neglected is the revenue and audience development potential of programs. The Philadelphia Zoo Treehouse troupe raised over $500,000 each year for the zoo; and Alberta Adamson of the Wheaton History Center reports that its programs grew from eleven in 1995 to ninety-five in 2003, with the audience more than doubling from 2,043 in 2000 to 4,207 in 2003. According to research conducted by Chicago teachers, "the Wheaton History Center was the only institution offering a powerful program on these subjects [the Underground Railroad, slavery, and abolition]."

■ ■ ■

The strongest recommendation I can make regarding how to sell the idea of museum theatre is to "show rather than tell." How can one show a program that does not yet exist? First, don't attempt to do it alone. Assuming that you have a style in mind for your museum theatre programs—for example, historical monologues, one-person puppet shows, storytelling—find a partner who can create a living example for you. Frequently, theatre groups or students of theatre will gladly collaborate with a museum for little or no cost if it might lead to future employment. If, for example, you intend to perform a puppet show for preschoolers in a museum gallery or as part of an exhibit, write and produce a prototype that you can present to those you are trying to persuade. Whenever possible, test the program first with the intended audience. In this case, invite a preschool to a rehearsal (you can compensate them with a free museum pass), and also have a preschool group present at the actual performance. There is no substitute for viewing the real thing and witnessing its effect on audiences.

Theatre revolves around emotion, and actors are highly skilled at evoking it in themselves and in their audiences. We best remember those things we have most strongly felt. As Lee Oestreicher writes, "Artists are useful because they grasp the community by the lapels and pull it, roughly or seductively, into the arena of feelings and ideas."[10] If we want museum visitors to learn about conflicts and upheavals in the lives of scientists, artists, historical figures, and ordinary people—and remember them later—we need to move our audience. Not every theatre piece needs to leave an audience in tears; there are many emotions apart from sadness. There is its opposite, joy (expressed by laughter or exuberance); anger (indignation or resentment at the fate of a character we've come to care about); and curiosity (satisfied or piqued).

One of the most compelling exercises I have seen for demonstrating the effectiveness of emotion and learning was developed by Randy Taylor of the International Museum of Art and Design in Atlanta, Georgia. This exercise can be conducted by a skilled educator with a group of between five and twenty people of any age. It has been well described by Paul Taylor of the Philadelphia Zoo:

> One experience, which effected a deep sense of transformation on many levels, was an exercise I participated in at the theatre workshop while at the Science Museum of Minnesota. The activity began as he [Randy Taylor] told all of us in the room that we were going to pretend to be archeologists. He gave us some prep on what an archeologist does, and then opened a large box.

The box contained reproductions of artifacts found in an Inca tomb. They included articles of clothing, food, toys, pots, jewelry, small figures, and some articles whose apparent use or function was not readily apparent. Randy

> carefully arranged them on the ground on a blanket. We were each given the task to select one of the artifacts and study it. We then had to relay our research to the group and tell everyone in detail what the artifact was and how it was used. There was a clear sense of play and at the same time a feeling that we were a group of colleagues sharing our findings. We pieced together through the artifacts that they were all from the burial site of a young girl.

When this part of the exercise was concluded, Randy asked the group to change from being archaeologists to friends of the young girl. They were asked to remember her, and to return the artifact to her grave accompanied with a story that connected it, the girl, and the narrator. "The sense of transformation in space, mood, and point of view was tremendous. As each of us told our story and placed the artifact where we had found it there was a deep sense of reverence."

I conducted this same exercise at the first Theatre in Museums Workshop held in South America, at the Museo de Historia Natural in Montevideo, Uruguay. I utilized the grave site concept, but with local indigenous artifacts, and, at first, I thought the exercise was not going to work. When asked to choose an object and describe its use, many of the participants used the moment to engage in humor, each trying to top the other in outlandish uses for their object. There was no sense of reverence and not much creativity being displayed. Far from sure that the second half of the exercise would succeed, I allowed the laughter and banter to die down, and then invited the group to change from anthropologists to friends of the dead person. I asked them to spend a few moments silently thinking about the object, its relationship to the dead person, and what they wanted to tell us.

By the time the first participant came forward to replace his object in the tomb, the mood in the room had already changed, and his quiet, simple story set the tone for the others. From then on the stories that were offered with the objects were highly imaginative, moving, and very personal. Some people were crying as they came forward, others cried as they listened to other people's stories. The transformation was complete, and the effect of personalizing objects and humanizing them with a story registered profoundly with all the participants.

One of the more moving experiences I have had with the power of theatre involved a play by Timothy Cope called *Starvation Winter*. The play is set in 1883 and was done in conjunction with SMM's exhibit After the Buffalo Were Gone. The play addresses the situation that developed at the Blackfeet Indian Reservation at Birch Creek, Montana, when promised supplies ran low and the Indians began to die of starvation. By the spring of 1884, almost one-quarter of the Blackfeet on the reservation had perished. The confrontation in the play is between two historical characters—Indian Agent Major John W. Young, and Almost-A-Dog, a Blackfeet elder who recorded the deaths on a notched willow stick. As Young admits to Almost-A-Dog, "The ranchers want your land. They think you have too much. They think the Reservation is too large. They think you can't be civilized so they have a better right to the land than you. They want to graze their cattle on it." Almost-A-Dog thinks this a sad joke. "Civilized!" he says.

> What does that word mean? It means act like white people. We are to pretend that cattle are like buffalo and we are like you. Well, that is not the truth. Cattle are not like buffalo! You could put your cows out on the prairie and treat them like buffalo for a hundred years, but they would not turn into buffalo. It is the same with red men. Even if we tried to live like white people, we would still be

different. We would still be red. My people know this and so do yours. What a
good trick the Great Spirit has played on us Blackfeet, eh? Once we needed the
white man for nothing. Now we need him for everything. Now that we have
nothing, the white man thinks we have too much.

As the time when the play was scheduled to open approached, Cope was
concerned. The Native American Advisory Council that had overseen the development of the exhibit and reviewed the draft of the play was scheduled to
be at the opening performance. The cast consisted of Steve Lick, an experienced museum theatre performer, as Major Young, and Bruce Murray, an An-
ishinabe performer best known in the Twin Cities for his comic routines, as
Almost-A-Dog. The performance took place in a cabin built into the exhibit
itself, with benches for seating. As the audience gathered, we were rather concerned to see a child of three or four take a seat in the front row, surrounded
by people of all ages, mainly adults. *Starvation Winter* is one of the few SMM
productions employing the fourth wall stage convention, making it virtually
impossible, once the play begins, for the actors to stop. The entire audience,
including the child, proved to be quiet and attentive.

At the end of the presentation, the actors took their bow, made some closing statements about the outcomes of the situations presented in the play, and
asked if there were any questions. Quite frequently, audiences take time for-
mulating their thoughts, but not that day. The child in the front row who had
initially concerned us spoke up at once, saying only one word. "Share!"

If we had ever had any doubts about the power of our medium, they were
dispelled in that moment. The Native American Advisory Council was almost
as brief, and their statement equally affirming. They simply said, "We've been
waiting one hundred years for someone to tell that story."

■ ■ ■

We began this chapter with a reminder of the value of entertainment in the
service of education, and went on to examine how theatre can draw attention
to and create interest in objects and topics that might otherwise be overlooked. At the core of the argument for adopting this technique is its appeal
to the emotions. We are all aware that events that move or touch us tend to
linger in our memory.

Understanding whom we're selling an idea to is essential to any plan. I have
seen excellent presentations fail only because emphasis was placed incorrectly.

For example, a colleague presented his idea for a museum theatre program to a board of directors composed primarily of Latinos and African Americans. He emphasized the entertainment aspect of the program more than its educational value and found that his proposal met with only mild enthusiasm. The board loved the idea of using music, dance, and masks, and thought the concept of employing professional actors a viable one, but they were concerned about how to market the program in their communities, where education is highly valued. When entertainment was deemphasized in the service of education, the proposal received the board's full support. This is not to suggest that all Latinos or all African Americans serving on boards would respond the same way. There are nevertheless cultural biases and traditions that it is valuable to be aware of before approaching a group or a board with a proposal for a museum theatre program.

NOTES

1. Gard was then theatre director for the institution.

2. Brown, *Museum News*, March 1964, quoted in Gard, "Entertainment in Education: A Justification," *Museum Theatre Journal* 2 (1994).

3. Gard, "Entertainment in Education."

4. Gonzales, "Museum Theatre Expands Texas Culture," *Museum Theatre Journal* (Spring 1995).

5. Forbes, "Museum Theater."

6. Winslow, "Theater at the Pittsburgh Children's Museum," *Museum Theatre Journal* (1994).

7. Duganne, "Witte Museum."

8. At the Science Museum of Minnesota.

9. Breckenridge, "The Heart Strings of Science," *Museum Theatre Journal* 9 (Fall/Winter 2000/2001).

10. Oestreicher, "Museum Theater."

Promoting and Marketing Your Theatre Program

There are three audiences to take into an account for a successful promotional effort for museum theatre programs: 1) the institution's board of directors, staff, volunteers, and members; 2) visitors (including schools); and 3) the media.

An effective way of keeping the first group—those already involved with the institution—informed, and of gaining their support, is to invite them to performances, even planning special events designed for them at which programs can be featured. These events can include backstage visits—chats with the actors, a presentation from the costumer on how a historical costume was designed and made, or a tour of the prop storage area.

Patricia Decker, director of programs for Explora, has found that members of the board of directors play an important part in promoting the theatre program by talking about it at meetings they attend throughout the city and by inviting others to come and see the performances. Decker reports that she has "often witnessed key directors of local, large businesses, city council members, U.S. senators, and state representatives sitting in the audience with (and sometimes without) their children, grandchildren, and other family members, enjoying our theatre programs." Staff at Explora believe that visitors who attend their theatre programs are their most effective promoters. "One visitor," reports Decker, "even wrote a 'Letter to the Editor' about how our play affected her nine-year-old son's understanding of history, art, and the culture and time of the Renaissance." A monthly calendar, which includes the theatre performances, is sent to museum members, with a follow-up postcard every time a new explorer is featured in the Great Explorer Series. Within the museum itself, signs provide information about the performance.

At SMM, special member events include one that features theatre performances, a backstage tour, and conversations with the actors, covering such topics as the development of scripts and the differences between performing at a traditional theatre and in a museum.

The Philadelphia Zoo Treehouse programs are promoted to members through the zoo's quarterly newsletter, which reaches fifty-five thousand homes. The birthday party program is advertised monthly in two family newspapers. Flyers are handed out at zoo events. Job listings and some promotion for the programs also appear on the local theatre community website.

Promotion aimed at visitors can include program announcements over the speaker systems, posters, and signboards with photos of the actors and of the performance. If a roster of events is being offered, a small printed program can be provided with the times and locations of the performances.

Including programs in the price of admission offers a wonderful opportunity to stress the value-added aspect of these offerings. This value can be communicated most effectively by greeters, ticketing staff, and information booth and floor staff, especially if they themselves have had an opportunity to enjoy the programs and are familiar with them.

The Whitaker Center believes that "there is no better marketing tool than word of mouth. At the end of every in-house performance, the actors inform the audience that our outreach Whitaker on Wheels (WOW) travels to their schools. The same is done at the end of the outreach show, encouraging the audience to visit us at Whitaker Center."

A handwritten sign outside the Ontario Science Centre auditorium advertising "A one-half hour zany comedy about science starring Ptolemy, Plato, and Copernicus" attracted seventeen thousand visitors in two weeks.

At many museums, including the SMM and the Buffalo Bill Historical Center, actors stay behind after performances to answer questions, which may be about the content of the piece or about an actor's costume or makeup. When puppets are used, they are sometimes brought out for children to see up close. (It is my opinion that this is best done by keeping the puppet "alive" or active, not displayed as another prop.) These sessions provide actors with an opportunity of promoting other programs that are being offered that day or new programs opening in the near future. Serkownek tells us that at the Buffalo Bill Historical Center actors

> also distribute handouts developed by the curators (often in conjunction with performers) which highlight the relationship between the performance and museum exhibits. Each handout includes a short biography to encourage visitors to further explore the program's topic. . . . At the Minnesota Historical Society, interpreters portraying characters based on historical persons hand visitors small pieces of paper which serve as both informative post-visit materials and as souvenirs of the encounter. On one side of the handout is an item that the character might be likely to give to someone. An interpreter portraying Minnesota's first public school teacher gives out a Reward of Merit card; another portraying an important African-American entrepreneur hands out an advertisement for her business. The other side of the handout gives a brief historical biography of the character.

Information about the Whitaker's programs is sent "to teachers and schools in the form of Educator's Guides and WOW Brochures." The Whitaker has also created the position of communications manager. This person "travels to the schools and meets with curriculum directors, teachers, school boards, and PTO/PTAs to showcase the programs."

The Carnegie markets its school outreach programs with a brochure, and the program specialist visits principals and teachers to promote the program.

In promotion to the press, event calendars, and radio and television programs, the value-added component can again be stressed. The book review editor of the *Albuquerque Journal*, a daily morning paper, often writes previews of Explora's theatrical offerings; and programs are listed in several magazines with city and statewide coverage. The Science Museum of Virginia lists performances in all local publications. A yearly paid ad is placed in an annual publication dedicated to local performance groups, and occasional advertising is purchased in the local papers. Opening night receptions are held for MainStage productions. In exchange for ticket and museum membership giveaways, the local public radio station provides regular mentions of the Science Museum of Virginia's productions. Flyers are distributed at libraries and community events.

Members of the press are regularly invited to performances at the Museo de Historia Natural, and accept the invitations. The program has been featured on one educational and two commercial television channels and has received write-ups in the newspapers. In addition, since it depends on state funding, the Museo has made sure that the various agencies regulating both the educational content and the budget for the museum receive regular bulletins on its progress and results, including personal appearances and presentations from the director of the program and of the museum. Heads of these agencies in turn visit the museum.

The Whitaker enjoys the support of its marketing department, which develops relationships with local papers and TV stations to get promotional pieces and publicity put before the public. A partnership with WGAL-TV Weather ensures that programs inside the Harsco Science Center as well as Whitaker on Wheels are showcased.

The Weisman often prepares a postcard mailer for special theatre events and sends it to a wider list than their members. "We sometimes do paid advertising in the student newspaper or one of the weeklies. We send press releases to local publications in hopes that they will list them in their calendars of events or give them an 'A' list notice or 'best bet.'"

The question of whether or not to encourage reviewers to see museum theatre offerings elicits a variety of responses from museums. While museum theatre practitioners maintain high standards for their productions, there are significant differences between performing in a museum and in a regular theatre, and most museums lack confidence that a theatre reviewer will take these differences into account. For this reason, most institutions prefer publicity to formal reviews.

There is unanimous agreement that the most effective promotion and marketing takes place within the institution, in the form of creating support for the theatre programs and encouraging everyone who comes into contact with visitors to promote them.

11

How Theatre Has Been Used to Present Difficult Issues

Plays thrive on conflict. The same cannot be said of most human beings, particularly those on an outing to a museum. For this reason, institutions often shy away from presenting difficult issues to their visitors. The experiences related in this chapter reveal that so long as certain guidelines are followed, rather than turning visitors off, presenting them with challenging and difficult information and situations can be immensely thought provoking and stimulating.

As was addressed in chapter 1, people who work in museums tend to be thoughtful and idealistic. We want our visitors to be exposed to ideas, to grapple with them, and even to use their knowledge for the greater good of society. The use of drama as a tool for social change has a history almost as long as the theatre itself. In the United States, theatre as an educational technique and one that would bring about change came into its own during the Great Depression, with the establishment in 1935 of the Federal Theatre Project, providing work for unemployed theatre professionals. The FTP's director, Hallie Flanagan, believed in the Federal Theatre "not merely as a decoration but a vital force in our democracy."[1]

The 1960s saw the beginning of a revolution in the research and the teaching of history, with the recognition that history should not concern itself only with generals, presidents, and conquerors (typically white male figures) but also with ordinary people and everyday events. As anthropologist Gilbert Wilson says in the play named after him, "History isn't just wars and battles and who got to be president or king or queen. History is the way we planted our corn and the songs we sang to make it grow."[2]

Dissatisfaction with the way museums were telling the human story ranged from history museums being criticized for portraying a conflict-free past, to anthropology and natural history museums being accused of ignoring the sometimes exploitative relationship between subject and collector. Art museums were attacked for showing the works of "a few elite, culturally canonized individuals."[3] Colonial Williamsburg and Plimoth Plantation both responded to these criticisms by creating new programs designed to include African American history and more realistic interpretations of the experiences of Pilgrims, and by addressing racial issues and temperance in their programs. History and science centers, natural history museums, and zoos followed suit, with programs that examined the ethics of collecting and the repatriation of religious artifacts and human remains. One of the tools they used was museum theatre.

In 1979, in the publication *A Stage for Science,* ASTC noted that "theatre is fiction to which the audience consents, and thus it can provide a nonthreatening framework for dealing with complex, crucial social issues relating to science. Theater makes it safe to contemplate disturbing controversies and to probe attitudes towards science."[4] The same is true for nonscientific subjects.

Paul Taylor of the Philadelphia Zoo Treehouse says that "some of the most powerful museum theatre productions are those that have dealt with controversial issues." He believes that such performances are particularly important at zoos and aquariums, where it is essential not only to "raise questions and ask people to reflect on their behavior," but also to "give them ways that they can contribute."

The Hidalgo County Historical Society has engaged high school students in the presentation of difficult subjects with a production of *Corazones morados* (Purple Hearts), addressing the painful historical inequity of social alienation and segregation.[5]

The Rochester Museum and Science Center (RMSC) decided to create a total immersion experience concerning the day that Frederick Douglass delivered, as Victoria Sandwick Schmitt puts it,

> what many historians believe is the most important anti-slavery oration of the nineteenth century. We designed *Meet Rochester's Abolitionists* as a school program for students in grades three through twelve. . . . We all agreed that RMSC's half-

century-old historic Rochester period rooms would provide an outstanding theatre set. Created during the Colonial Revival era, these dioramas are peopled with wax figures. If we augmented the figures with live actors, we could make them come alive as authentic settings for events from the days of the Underground Railroad.

Scenes took place in a tin shop, the general store, a kitchen, and a drug store, peopled with live actors interacting with visitors.

We created a scenario in which students would become Rochester abolitionists, gathered to hear the great orator give his speech. They encounter Frederick Douglass by accident "on the street" and then make their way through town to Corinthian Hall to hear the speech, meeting some of Douglass' friends and fellow workers on the Underground Railway en route.

The characters included Isaac and Amy Post, active in the abolitionist and the women's rights movements, and Sojourner Truth. After the performance, the actors put aside their characters and spoke to the audience, and all paid a visit to the RMSC's library, where they could view photographs of the period and see a real Underground Railroad pass, as well as Douglass's signed copy of his speech. "A recent educators' survey revealed that a number of educators rated seeing *Meet Rochester's Abolitionists* and visiting the museum archives as being among the best field trips they have ever experienced anywhere. . . . In February 2002, the show was offered to the general public. Much to everyone's surprise the presentation drew two thousand people for twenty shows."

The Kentucky History Center took on racism and violence with its play *Red, White, and Black (The Bradens, the Wades and a Bombing)*. It presents the story of an African American couple who buy a house in the 1950s in an all-white neighborhood. A few months later, their home is bombed and the couple accused of having done it themselves in order to incite racial tension. Thirty years later, a similar incident occurred. LaVoie writes, "One family. . . hesitated bringing their father to the show because of his 'bigoted' attitudes, but the performance made such an impact on him that he returned to see the show a second time. The father told the museum staff that the play caused him to reflect on how he had lived his life and, he remarked, 'It shook me.'"[6]

At SMM, *Genetic Prophecy: Do You Really Want to Know?* by Judy MacGuire was developed for a new exhibit on human biology. The exhibit team chose to use the theatre format to explain a serious genetic disorder for which genetic testing could be conducted. The disorder selected was Huntington's Disease (HD), a progressive disorder of the brain and central nervous system. The play calls for three actors, who portray two families and their counselors. The first family consists of a husband and wife. The wife decides to have the predictive test and discovers that she has indeed inherited the HD gene. Not only do she and her husband have to deal with the knowledge that she will gradually lose her faculties and enter a vegetative state, but they have to rethink their dream of having children. The husband wants to go ahead, the wife does not.

The second family consists of a brother and sister discussing their father's death. He carried the gene, and his two adult children argue about whether or not to be tested. One of them has lived an irresponsible and unhappy life, a result, he believes, of his assumption that he would one day die of HD. Now that a test is available he wonders what he will do if the results should prove negative. His sister, who has married and had two children, has decided that her life would not change either way, and refuses to be tested.

The role of the counselor is designed to provide transitional and factual information about the disease and its effects. The counselor reveals that HD is a crippling and deadly disease, caused by a gene inherited from a parent. The chances of inheriting HD are fifty-fifty, and in 1993, the specific gene responsible for HD was discovered, leading to a predictive genetic test.

The play was presented for a total of 267 performances over a three-year period, and audiences responded to it positively, seriously considering the question asked at the end of the play: "But would you really want to know?" Few felt able to categorically answer yes or no, most wanted time to think about it or believed that circumstances would determine their choice, but all wondered and considered. Most were unaware of HD and had many questions about the disease itself. Those who had experience of the disease took the opportunity to share personal stories.

Actors reported that audience members who remained in the theatre after the performance were usually debating the question of whether or not they would choose to have the test, or had personal anecdotes to share. Exhibit staff told of hearing ongoing discussions after audience members left the theatre.

A second SMM piece, addressing the difficult issue of human population, was *The More the Scarier*, by Amy Ward. Script development began as a series of workshops and discussions with the playwright, five actors, and the director. The goal was to establish an atmosphere of trust and honesty as feelings, assumptions, and biases were examined. There were two major reasons why this was important. One was that the cast itself was a microcosm of audiences at large. The second reason was that actors would be answering questions after each performance and needed to examine what their reactions to some of these questions might be. All the actors who performed the piece agreed that if a script had been handed to them ready-made, they could have learned their lines and performed their parts. They emphasized, however, that in a museum theatre setting that includes the question-and-answer format, it would have been very difficult for them to do it well without a personal commitment to the material.

Ongoing research and guest speakers were part of the initial process. The actors described the research on human population as "dreadful," "hopeless," and "depressing." Nothing positive seemed to emerge. Steve Flamm, an actor also privately involved with the Hunger Project (whose goal was to end hunger by the year 2000), wanted to believe that hunger, at least, was a matter of distribution of resources. Only the overwhelming impact of the figures he found on soil erosion and water depletion convinced him otherwise. Representatives from various organizations, holding polarized points of view, visited us. At one extreme, we heard that the earth could comfortably maintain forty billion humans; at the other, that every pregnancy is a problem.

I have learned the value of encouraging and supporting playwrights and actors as they work through issues, often spending rehearsal time writing and rehearsing portions of a script that may not be included in the final version. Actor Paul Short said of the process, "Never before have I felt such a strong singularity of mind in the midst of such varying points of view, and, at times, such apparent chaos."

In this case, the further we went into the topic, the more we realized that the information we would be asking our audiences to absorb was literally life threatening. Amy Ward asked us all to give up something as evidence of the fact that we understood the seriousness of the topic. We were all surprised by what we were willing to offer. One of us became a vegetarian, another gave up buying new clothes, another traveling for pleasure, and another having children. In a follow-up conducted four years later, we found that these commitments had all been kept.

The final result of our efforts was a musical. It contained humor, dance, and singing, and the information was conveyed via a series of human situations and choices, some sad, some humorous.

About five hundred audience members were surveyed. Questions ranged from "Would you like us to present more issues of this kind?" (to which we received 499 responses of "Yes") to asking whether the information presented might lead the person to make any changes in his or her lifestyle. Answers were thoughtful and profound, including one from a ten-year-old: "I might have only one kid when I grow up."

The Science Museum of Virginia's Carpenter Theatre Company produced a play titled *Take Two*, addressing the plight of a high school student who discovers that he or she (the part can be played by an actress or an actor) has a diseased heart and needs a heart transplant in order to survive. The play examines how family and friends confront the issue from religious perspectives, and how they deal with the fact that there is a long waiting list and that the majority of people on it die before a replacement organ becomes available.

The Lawrence Hall of Science presented *The Story of Itiba*, about the genocide of the Taino people in the wake of Columbus's voyages. "The play," Dornfest says, "was cast with and codirected by First Nation [Native American] peoples," and it was developed with their participation.

With a grant received from the California Department of Health Services, Tobacco Control Section, the Lawrence Hall of Science also examined the subject of smoking. The department had emphasized that it "wanted to utilize theatre to generate controversy and discussion about tobacco amongst middle and high school students." Naomi Stein explains,

As we are associated with the University of California, it was important to balance that desire with the tradition of nonadvocacy embraced by the University. One way this was handled was by creating a website that holds additional information and links to other resources, so that teachers are enabled to continue discussion of "hot topics" in a supported manner. We partnered with the local tobacco education counselors at schools so that they were present at the shows and could continue conversations that the play generated. Another tactic applied towards handling the issues responsibly were focus groups to understand our audience and to learn what they wanted to know. These findings indicated that the youth in our area were intelligent and particularly sensitive to being condescended to. Therefore the creative team . . . focused on these three issues: the role of peer pressure in a teen's decisions about tobacco, the tobacco industry's attempts to market to youth, and the effects of the industry in developing nations. In the*Boardroom of Big Tobacco* the author chose to script the CEO's speech entirely out of direct quotes from the tobacco industry and put the script online so that any viewer could "click" on the quotes and go to the original source. This was very effective; many students commented that this objective source legitimized the information portrayed in the play. Also in this story line an ad is dissected to show the inherent manipulative elements, with media literacy sites linked on the website. The story line about developing nations was played entirely in mask and movement with voiceovers of facts (also online) that put the fictional story in a factual context. In the story line about peer pressure, the protagonist never makes a decision but rather leaves the viewers with an open-ended question: "What are you gonna do?" Whenever a school's schedule allowed, the show was followed with the website. The partnership with teachers and the focus groups allowed us to create controversy responsibly.

The guidelines that emerged for working with difficult or controversial subjects are as follows:

- Make every effort to ensure that the information presented is well documented and researched.
- Confrontations and discussions should occur between characters, not between performers and their audience.
- Make sure that the audience feels invited to consider the issue from various perspectives.

One of the strengths of theatre is that it allows us to give voice to several points of view—as part of the performance, characters can reveal how they have come to hold these diverse opinions and how and why they may have changed.

It is profoundly rewarding to watch the delight, excitement, and occasional dismay of people of all ages engaged in examining their preconceptions, their biases and prejudices, and discovering their own extraordinary capacity for change.

NOTES

1. Flanagan, quoted in Serkownek, "Museum Theatre."

2. From SMM's play *Gilbert Wilson*, by Steven Flamm.

3. Serkownek, "Museum Theatre."

4. ASTC, *Stage for Science.*

5. Oliver Franklin, "The Large in the Small of It: How a Small Museum Uses Theatre to Enlarge Its Advantages," *Museum Theatre Journal* 4 (Spring 1996).

6. LaVoie, "To Engage."

Collaborations
and Partnerships

Several museums have explored collaborations with other educational institutions and theatre providers, describing most of them as extremely positive. Some of these collaborations have been stressful but ultimately turned out well, and a few have not worked out at all.

We will begin by examining a project that did not have a happy outcome. The parties involved wish to remain anonymous but are very willing to share what they learned from the experience. Institution A was seeking to develop a demonstration using theatrical techniques. Believing that an experienced director and playwright who had worked together successfully on other projects would be their best choice, they approached such a team about the project, presenting it to them as a theatre project. *From this initial vocabulary most of the ensuing problems resulted.*

The playwright and director did not live in the area, and, due to their reputation and experience, they were hired for the project *without being invited to visit the institution first.* With hindsight, institution A now knows that had it invited them and incurred this additional expense many of the misunderstandings that later arose could have been avoided. It believes that a site visit would have provided everyone involved with an opportunity to introduce the institution to the writer and director, and to test the chemistry of the personalities involved.

The writer and director in turn feel that had they done a site visit, they would have sensed immediately that leadership at institution A was tenuous and not clearly defined, and *that it was not a play that was wanted, but a demonstration.* As examined by Susan Wolsfeld in her article "Learning from Experience: The Only Rewrite Life Permits," "the responsibility of coordinating a plethora of egos, ambitions, and goals" (which in this case fell on the shoulders of the guest director and a staff member at the institution) "can diffuse the focus of the project rendering its creative process challenging at best, and nightmarish at worst, and its success less probable, if not impossible."[1]

No single person was identified by institution A as the decision maker, leaving the script open to comment, criticism, and revision by ten staff and senior management who dropped in and out of the script revision sessions at various times, often expressing contradictory opinions. Not surprisingly, an acceptable script was not produced, egos were bruised, and resources wasted.

The next example is of a project that did ultimately come to fruition, but not without a number of missteps.

THE MINNESOTA HISTORICAL SOCIETY (MHS), IN THE HEART OF THE BEAST PUPPET AND MASK THEATRE, AND MHS'S INDIAN ADVISORY COMMITTEE

The Minnesota Historical Society was preparing to open a new exhibit called Manoominikewin: Stories of Wild Ricing, developed with an Indian Advisory Committee that included tribal community leaders, elders, and scholars from throughout the state. A puppet show depicting a wild rice origin story was planned to accompany the opening of the exhibit. As described by Wendy Jones, the Historical Society's interpretative programs supervisor, "the original goal was to use a puppet show to convey the elements of ritual, tradition, and spiritual significance in wild ricing. Our target audience would be families with small children."

In the Heart of the Beast Puppet Theatre was hired to create three short plays, and

> out of respect for the wishes of our advisory board, we had agreed to perform the wild ricing origin story only when snow was on the ground. Thinking that there might be times when no snow had fallen by the date of a pre-advertised program, we felt the need for a back up. Thus the other two pieces commissioned were nonorigin stories about a day of ricing. In the Heart of the Beast completed its contractual obligation, and we presented the final draft of the script to our advisory committee.... The consensus was that it was not ready to be performed. Al-

though the play had been written by an Ojibwe actor/playwright, the advisory committee questioned the respectfulness and authenticity of its "voice." The language and tone of the play, the descriptions of harvesting wild rice, and the context of some of its Ojibwe words did not seem appropriate. Who, they asked, was the playwright? With what band of Ojibwe was he affiliated? How old was he? They did not know him. Some members, upon seeing the script, started to question whether or not it was appropriate to tell the origin story at all.

The exhibit opened without the puppet show, which did not see the light of day until "more than five years after it first received the 'go-ahead' from the Minnesota Historical Society's exhibits and education departments and its Indian Advisory Committee. Obviously," Jones says, "we had brought our advisory committee into the process much too late. We also learned that when you hire someone from a community to tell its story, you need to make sure that the rest of the community agrees that he is the best person for the job."[2]

At the other end of the spectrum are several collaborations that were essentially problem free.

Manoomin Stories: A Wild Ricing Puppet Show *by Chris Warren with adaptations by Jim Northrup, performed by Julie Kastigar and Dawn Reed. Photograph reprinted with permission of the Minnesota Historical Society.*

MISSOURI HISTORICAL SOCIETY
AND HISTORYONICS THEATRE COMPANY

Jim Powers, the former Community Programs director at the Missouri Historical Society, wanted to find a way to better serve schools and reach a larger audience among the general public. The society's mission is to demonstrate how the threads of the past weave with the present, and in October 1993, when an exhibit about the Gilded Age opened there, Powers and Larry Roberson determined that "a theatrical piece could be an important vehicle for the museum to interpret such issues as racism, poverty, and crime—issues with roots in the Gilded Age."[3] For help with this idea, Powers approached the Historyonics Theatre Company. It was agreed that Historyonics would create "brief vignettes that could be presented in the gallery space, making live theatre part of the total exhibit experience. The vignettes would be presented on a rotating schedule on weekends and special occasions." The museum hired the playwright, and the theatre company hired and rehearsed the actors, also "commissioning the creation of period costumes, and assembling the necessary props to mount the vignettes." The project was hailed as a complete success, with the vignettes reaching sixty-three hundred visitors during approximately six months of performances. Not only did the vignettes appeal to visitors and receive "a rush of attendance from schools," but the project also received a state award.

Historyonics moved its offices into the Missouri Historical Society (MHS) and became "the theatre in residence" there. Both organizations, however, retain their separate identities. "In addition to its contract work for the historical society," Powers says, "Historyonics now produces its mainstage season of four shows at the MHS Library and Collections Center auditorium." They are also

> collaborating on an outreach program that takes historical performances to schools and other groups. Included are *Call Me Out My Name*, a show about freed slaves in Saint Louis; *The Web of Life*, a storytelling piece about the Hopi Tribe; and *When Trains Reigned*, about the heyday of trains. Collaboration is shared creation. It involves shared responsibility, shared trust and shared resources. It takes time and hard work, but it allows two or more groups to accomplish that which they would never be able to accomplish alone.

THE SCIENCE MUSEUM OF MINNESOTA AND
THE UNIVERSITY OF NORTH CAROLINA

The university had been seeking an internship opportunity with a strong emphasis on educational theatre for its performance arts students, while the museum had experienced personnel cuts that reduced its performing staff. The two institutions agreed that it would be mutually beneficial for the university to provide performing and playwrighting interns with actual work experience in educational theatre by sending them to SMM for eight to ten weeks during the summer months to rehearse and perform in demonstrations and plays.

One of the challenges was that neither the university nor the museum had funds to pay for travel or housing. This challenge was addressed by asking interns to pay for their own travel expenses and providing them with housing when they arrived. SMM staff generously hosted the interns during their stay.

THE FRANKLIN INSTITUTE AND THE
AMERICAN HISTORICAL THEATRE (AHT)

As described by Bill Sommerfield of the AHT,

> Some years ago, the Franklin Institute . . . received a grant from IBM to exhibit models of Leonardo da Vinci's inventions. . . . To enhance the exhibit, AHT wrote a thirty minute "play" suited to restricted performance in a simple replica of Leonardo's laboratory. Two "Leonardos" were rehearsed and costumed, each to perform three times on alternate days. . . . A wide range of audience, over 23,000 people, young and old, attended and even more exciting, many spent time afterwards perusing the models of inventions encased in glass. AHT subsequently received a contract to direct a video of the play for release to other science museums. In addition, AHT ran a full-day seminar for the volunteer docents and staff of the Franklin Institute on how to incorporate theatrical techniques into scientific demonstrations and lectures.[4]

The American Historical Theatre also collaborated with the Boston Public Library and the Bicentennial Commission for the U.S. Constitution. (These examples are included here because both projects could just as readily have taken place in a museum.) Public relations staff at the Boston Public Library wished to conduct tours. As described by Sommerfield,

Since few of the staff had ever guided tours before, the first day of the training period was devoted to basic presentational skills. During the second day, advice about how theatrical elements would give the stories extra life and vibrancy was presented in cameo stories about the artists, architects and early library staff (the runners wearing white gloves who fetched the books on request). Vignettes were introduced and critiqued. Within the allowable historic framework, each docent developed stories he/she liked best and was encouraged to add his or her own "voice." Docents stepped into first person, assuming the character, voice or even dialect of the persona in focus. . . . By the end of the day docents eagerly donned small pieces of costuming (a long skirt, a pair of white gloves) to make themselves stand out from the library visitors.[5]

In 1989 the Bicentennial Commission for the U.S. Constitution

selected AHT to train and interpret the role of George Washington during the re-creation of our first President's journey to his inauguration. The seven day journey from Mount Vernon to New York had to be meticulously researched and historically accurate with over forty presentations planned for the journey. Eighteenth-century costuming had to be exact as did style, speech and manners. The interpreter mastered the entire Washington biographical canon in order to answer questions from the press as if it were indeed 1789.[6]

THE IMMIGRANTS' THEATRE PROJECT AND THE SEAPORT MUSEUM

New York City's South Street Seaport Museum wanted to portray the period when most Irish, German, and Scandinavian immigrants arrived in the United States—between 1800 and 1860—and they approached the Immigrants' Theatre Project to create a series of plays on the subject. Work began with a tour of the Seaport Museum, followed by a month of negotiations. The Immigrants' Theatre Project prepared a time line and descriptions of the programs it proposed. Research and development began once it was agreed that the theatre would assume responsibility for the scripts and for the theatre staff required to execute them.

The scripts were described by the partners as "real-time" narratives, "with fifteen minutes of the performance being fifteen minutes in the lives of our immigrants." Topics covered were "the gruesome . . . long voyages aboard a cargo ship and the political, economic, and religious issues that prompted immigration."

Marcy Arlin, the theatre's artistic director, emphasized the importance of researching the performance site and who the audience would be. She concluded that the plays needed to be in simple English, because many of the audience members would be visiting from other countries. She also decided that the style of the scripts would be interactive and humorous to "accommodate the short attention spans of an audience easily distracted by the competing attractions of the ship's exhibit and the Seaport's buskers, weather, other tourists, police helicopters, spilled sodas, lost tourists, wayward children, Flying Elvises, and a hurricane."

The selection of actors was also influenced by the site, the audience, and the style that had now been determined. They were chosen "for strong voices that needed no outdoor amplification, experience improvising and interacting with an audience, appropriate ethnic background and/or a good accent."

THE PHILADELPHIA ZOO TREEHOUSE, AN AFTER-SCHOOL PROGRAM, AND A PROFESSIONAL PUPPET COMPANY

The Philadelphia Zoo Treehouse collaborated with an after-school program and a professional puppet company to create a show about urban animals to be presented by the school for the community. A professional puppeteer became artist in residence at the school for eight weeks, working with Treehouse staff twice a week to teach children about urban animals and create the show. Paul Taylor comments that "by far the greatest partnership that was formed was the one between the kids and ourselves. We did far more than create a show. We nurtured their individual talents and gave them a greater sense of self-worth." The majority of the children came from poor homes and without this project might have had little or no exposure to live theatre.

THE SCIENCE MUSEUM OF VIRGINIA AND THEATRE IV

The museum's Carpenter Science Theatre Program contracted Theatre IV, a children's theatre company, to produce and perform four productions with science themes for their series KidStage. Theatre IV, the second-largest touring company for children in the United States, offers two science-related shows to schools each year. "In return for free performances of these shows," Gard says, "the Science Museum of Virginia endorses the science content in the scripts and develops study guides for each."

Since the company is charged with providing live theatrical interpretation not only at the Science Museum of Virginia but also at its two satellite museums, the Danville Science Center and the Virginia Aviation Museum, the Science Museum of Virginia also partnered with Young Audiences of Virginia (YAV), which provided performances related to science and others that included dance, music, and poetry. In return for these performances, Gard explains, the Science Museum of Virginia renders a similar service to the one it offers Theatre IV. They review YAV scripts and endorse the science content. "A small amount of the Carpenter Science Theatre Company's annual budget has been dedicated to paying for a certain number of YAV performances at a reduced fee, and some of the performances have been free of charge."

CARNEGIE MUSEUM OF NATURAL HISTORY AND SHOP N' SAVE

A partnership between the Carnegie Museum of Natural History and Shop N' Save invited schools to save sales receipts from purchases made at the local Shop N' Save grocery store. When the requisite number of receipts had been saved, the school received a performance from the Carnegie's Science on Stage troupe. Michael List says that "this has been a great way for low-income-level school districts to get the program at no output of cash from the school. This partnership has done very well for both the museum and the grocery store chain [Super Valu]."

THE FIELD MUSEUM OF NATURAL HISTORY
AND SECOND CITY, CHICAGO

Bill Singerman, administrator of school partnerships at the Field Museum, was searching for ways in which to bring naturalistic dioramas to life. For almost six months, he took courses in improvisation at Second City, Chicago, realizing after his first class that there were connections between improvisational theatre and "the team-building and object-based activities employed in class." He also saw ways to use improvisation to bring objects and dioramas to life. Together, Second City and the Field Museum put together a course for teachers titled "Bringing Dioramas to Life." It was led by two Second City educators, took place at the Field Museum, and was open to teachers of all grades and disciplines. The teachers were divided into small groups of six to eight participants, and their first task was to examine a diorama of the famous Lions of Tsavo. This they did using a visual focus exercise, consisting of fo-

cusing first on a small aspect of the exhibit, then on a larger part of it, and, finally, on the entire diorama. After a brief discussion, the teachers were
asked—as a group—to perform an exercise called Part of a Whole, in which
they became parts of one of the animals in the diorama. "One teacher became
the body," Singerman reports,

> another, a leg, a third, the tail. Gradually, they worked as a team to become one
> unit—a human lion mirrored after the male specimen in the diorama. . . . They
> captured and orally described the ways in which the paws touch the ground, the
> way the mane and whiskers flare, the position held by the tail, etc. Next, teachers
> were divided into smaller groups. They were instructed to select a diorama fea-
> turing a number of animals posed in a naturalistic setting. Their task? To come
> up with three freeze frames—a before, during, and after. In other words, teach-
> ers had to create a story—what is happening in the diorama? What happened
> right before the animals were frozen? What will happen next? Some teachers
> came up with scenes in which animals were scouting for food, others were lis-
> tening for predators, some animals were teaching their young. In doing so, par-
> ticipants were able to bring the diorama to life; they were able to look beyond the
> animals frozen in time and think about how the animals' positioning, postures,
> and expressions inform us of their behaviors and environments. The response
> was overwhelmingly positive. Teachers discussed how this kind of activity could
> engage all kinds of learners, how it would help make students enthusiastic about
> exploring dioramas and how it would focus their students' attention effectively.[7]

Second City offers a professional development program called Improvisation for Creative Pedagogy, which assists teachers in adapting improvisational
exercises and techniques to any subject area. As a result of their experience
with the Field Museum, they also put together a resource booklet—*Improvisation for the Museum Experience*—addressing the use of improvisation in the
classroom, and with improvisational concepts, skills, and tips for integrating
improvisation with the museum field trip.

From this range of experience, the following key elements for success
emerged:

▪ Clarity of purpose: Why is the collaboration being sought? How is each
  party benefiting from or supporting the work of the other?

- Definition of expectations for both parties
- Establishment of a decision-making process
- A time line for the achievement of each step in the collaboration
- A contract or detailed letter of agreement

NOTES

1. Wolsfeld, "Learning from Experience: The Only Rewrite Life Permits," *Museum Theatre Journal* (April 1993).

2. Jones, "Telling a Story That Is Not Your Own: The Manoomin Stories," *Museum Theatre Journal* 5 (Fall 1997).

3. Powers and Roberson, "A Model for Collaboration," *Museum Theatre Journal* 3 (Spring 1995).

4. Sommerfield, "George Washington Lives: The Art of First Person Interpretation Enriches Traditional History Lessons," *Museum Theatre Journal* 3 (Spring 1995).

5. Sommerfield, "George Washington Lives."

6. Sommerfield, "George Washington Lives."

7. Singerman, correspondence with the author, December 12, 2003.

Historic Interpretation

History is not dry facts and dates, but a fabulous dramatic story that makes for great theater.

—*Wendy Jones, "Profile: Minnesota History Center"*

In her thesis on the relationship between museum theatre and living history, Robin LaVoie says that

> both aim to foster an emotional involvement with a museum's collections by providing a human context for the artifacts. These performances can equally provoke questions, promote active enjoyment, stimulate interest in the issues presented and encourage further investigation. Yet, there are some critical distinctions between the intent and structure of these approaches that make each unique. When the techniques are brought into the light, it becomes clear that one approach cannot adequately be used to describe the other.

LaVoie points out that reenactors, for example, "often speak in the third-person, concentrating more on the authenticity of dress, behaviors, and battle movements than on performing the role of a particular person from the past," and that first-person interpretation is "designed to offer interpreters as 'living artifacts.'" She also believes that "while both museum theatre and living history involve a person taking on a character in order to enhance the museum's overall message, the difference is in the *intent* of the performance." Her point is that

In the Fashion of the Country *by Eric Ferguson, performed by Shawn Hoffman and Melissa Whiteman. Photograph reprinted with permission of the Minnesota Historical Society.*

living history programs aim to create the feeling of having "just witnessed a reincarnation of real people from the past," while theatre—which she describes as a fictionalized representation—"provokes curiosity about that past."[1]

I propose that theatre programs do indeed aim to create the feeling in audiences that they have just witnessed and experienced something real. Both reenactments and dramatic presentations require the same suspension of disbelief. Audiences know that they are not really watching a battle or being spoken to by someone who has been dead for centuries, but the skill of both reenactors and actors lies in making audiences believe for a few moments that they have.

Ann F. Peabody, former supervisor of interpretation at the Mystic Seaport Museum, writes,

For many visitors to historic sites, there is nothing so rewarding as being involved in a personal experience with the past. Many historic sites utilize a variety of theatrical interpretation methods, from total immersion in a re-created experience, to individuals in character inter-mingled with third person interpretation, to scripted performances in formal theatrical settings. . . . No matter which interpretive methods a site decides work best, all educational theatre pieces begin with the research in an attempt to bring a loosely knit bundle of factual evidence to life.[2]

Peabody goes on to say that in creating the final program, there is no substitute for research.

It is, however, important to know what your objectives are before creating such a program. For instance, knowing what audience the program will predominantly serve helps to determine the depth to which your inquiry must go. . . . Educational objectives for the piece are also important to articulate before beginning the research: what do we want the viewer or participant to learn, or what emotions do we want to invoke in the audience? . . . Recording sources of information and indicating where they can be found helps those who may want to retrace a researcher's steps. . . . Writers and individuals working on a presentation in unscripted venues at historic sites need to monitor continually the balance between what is actually known, what is deduced from general source materials, and what is made up. . . . Theatre is particularly evocative as a tool in teaching social history, especially when the objective is to help people understand the nature of a particular time period. Topics, such as war, racism or politics, that are difficult to discuss because they evoke intense emotions, can be openly presented in a dramatic format. It is here that writers and role-players can use their special skills to round out and augment historic facts.[3]

LaVoie points out that theatre

can play with time to make visual comparisons between different eras. For example, a program at the Senator John Heinz Pittsburgh Regional History Center called *When He Was Gone* compared the experiences of a Civil War widow and a Vietnam War widow. In this short play, two paintings in a portrait gallery come to life and as they talk, they "help each other to grieve their lost husbands" and illustrate how the act of mourning has changed within our culture. Theatre can also illustrate history's connection to the present by making overt juxtapositions. The Kentucky History Center, for instance, presented *Red, White, and Black (The Bradens, the Wades and a Bombing)*, exploring a case of racially motivated violence in 1950s Kentucky. The performance touched on racial tensions in more recent memory as well by making explicit reference to a similar incident that occurred in Kentucky in 1985. Thus, by allowing characters to time travel within the play itself, or by bringing together characters who lived at different times, theatre can explore the nuances of historical change.[4]

At the Minnesota History Center several types of theatrical interpretation are offered, helping the museum "provide a place where people actively participate in finding personal meaning from things of the past." One is the History Players Program. As described by Wendy Jones, the History Players are staff interpreters who have spent months studying the intricate details of a historical figure's life and world. Although the interpreters speak as that character while interacting with visitors, they also acknowledge their present-day surroundings and use a modified first-person approach to compare and contrast time periods. They converse informally with visitors throughout the exhibits, but also periodically gather a crowd together in the performance space to tell a story about life in another time. In the words of Jones,

> Storytelling is frequently used to dramatize the people, places and events behind objects that would otherwise sit complacently in glass cases. Interactive skits called "History Bits" are used to demonstrate historical concepts, such as learning about the past through garbage. In *You Are What You Trash*, an interpreter hands visitors pieces of contemporary trash and asks them to draw conclusions about their own society based on what they see. Each of these programs asks visitors to think critically about past and present while connecting the themes to parallels in their own lives. Most importantly, however, the programs are fun.[5]

When asked what museum theatre does for the Minnesota History Center, Jones replied that theatre

- gives history an immediate voice;
- presents the ideas and feelings of history in the context of human behavior;
- fosters learning through participation;
- enables visitors to have a dialogue with the past;
- fosters empathy and "historical mindedness" in visitors of all ages;
- can be used to build relationships with communities;
- extends the "life" of an exhibit;
- easily adapts to diverse audience needs.

Claudia Pratt, outreach programs coordinator at the State Historical Society of North Dakota, describes her experiences this way:

As we know, museum theatre contrasts from living history in that it is scripted and dramatically performed for a certain period of time. Living history on the other hand is spontaneous and can be presented in first or third person. The Society taps a varied pool of writers—actors, playwrights, historians, educators, and community scholars. This has produced a variety of approaches and qualities of scripts. We constantly struggle with balancing historical accuracy and the use of dramatic license in portraying the characters. This season the Society developed guide-lines to improve the quality and process of developing the scripts. . . . To date, the program reaches approximately five percent of the site visitors through 130 plus performances each season. . . . The History Alive! program has thrived because our visitors like it, it is a high impact interpretive method, and is an economical way for the Society to provide quality programming at the sites.[6]

Bonnie Williams, curator of the Wylie House Museum in Bloomington, Indiana, writes this about her use of first-person interpretation:

Instead of transporting visitors back in time and pretending it's the 1840s, I bring a character from the 1840s into the present. . . . In this way, Flexible First-Person reduces the emphasis on the physical site and the artifacts themselves and focuses more attention on the historical narrative. . . . It also allows the interpreter to relate to the visitor's own world in ways which dramatically open avenues of communication and understanding. Anachronisms and anomalies which before were stumbling blocks become points of discussion about our changing culture. . . . When I greet the children, I am in costume but not in character. With the kids comfortably seated around me in the parlor, we talk about what a house museum is and how we learn what life was like long ago. Imagination, I tell them is part of the process. Imagination helps us to put ourselves in the historical picture, helps us see things from another perspective, ask new questions, understand things in a different way.[7]

In her presentation, the interpreter then wonders aloud what it would be like if the character she is portraying were to come to life and visit the group. She invites the children to close their eyes, and when they reopen them, greet the visitor. "The character is now 'on.'" Instead of being asked to participate in

a play, the children will play a game of pretending, making them "equal players with the interpreter. During the ensuing tour children are asked to imagine their own home being turned into a museum. The interpreter can answer
questions about historical anomalies." Williams points out that no class has
ever failed to notice the museum's motion sensors and ask about them. Her
answer, in character, is: "Do you know, I puzzled over that myself for the
longest time. It certainly wasn't here when I was a girl. Finally, I asked, and
what do you think? It's a burglar alarm! I suppose in my day our burglar alarm
was our dog. You know, they don't have a dog here anymore, so maybe they
need such gadgets." Answering questions in ways that relate to both the past
and the present, Williams believes, helps audiences to make connections and
enter "the stream of history."

At the other end of the interpretive spectrum are the actor/historians who
portray more than twenty different historical figures at the Pittsburgh Regional History Center. They are required to remain in character at all times,
during their thirty- to forty-five-minute monologue performances and when
they greet and talk with museum patrons and school tour groups. They have
also participated in History Face to Face, consisting of a brief play and a
question-and-answer period following it.

■ ■ ■

In her article "Living History in an Art Museum," Diane Brandt Stillman
states that

> every work of art was made by someone and for someone, embodying human
> creativity and beliefs and reflecting a way of life. Living history in an art mu-
> seum identifies the inherent drama in art through this human element, delving
> into the lives of those for whom the art was made, the social fabric surrounding
> the art, the beliefs of the people during the time the art was created, and the
> ideas on beauty that they held.

This could just as readily be applied to living history interpretation at a historic house or site, and the same is true of the criteria Brandt Stillman outlines for

> deciding which collections yield the greatest potential for living history per-
> formances. Collections that present the greatest opportunity to investigate is-

sues of patronage, symbolism, craftsmanship, esthetics, and social history are excellent candidates. . . . An art historical period that is far enough away in time to enable the actors to be dressed in interesting costumes is an obvious choice.[8]

Paul Taylor remarks that one wouldn't normally associate zoos with historical presentations, but at the Philadelphia Zoo an actress portrays the granddaughter of William Penn in the zoo's eighteenth-century house, Solitude. She relates the history of the house itself and of how a zoo came to be built around it.

With its outreach performances, Plimoth Plantation has tried a style of theatre called "conflict resolution drama." As examined by LaVoie, these dramas "take the dramatic portrayal of historical conflict a step further by allowing the students to actively question the characters' beliefs and values. In this format, a twenty-minute scripted scene between two characters reaches a 'crisis point,' at which time the actors turn to their audience for help." LaVoie uses the example of *I Would Be No Persecutor,* in which a Puritan woman is arrested and confronted by her father for marrying a Quaker in a secret ceremony. "Theatre's ability," LaVoie says,

to bring to life the emotional stakes of a conflict from a variety of perspectives helps museums to reveal the complexity of history in another way—by introducing difficult topics. . . the darker side of history. . . . Characters living "in the moment" reveal their terror, anger, pain or confusion to an audience that knows what will ultimately happen to them, helping visitors to understand the meanings and motivations that shape history.[9]

Some museums have even enhanced their collections with theatre—in the case of the Senator John Heinz Pittsburgh Regional History Center, by recording a collection of oral histories. The Historical Society of Western Pennsylvania developed a program called "History Face to Face," combining a performance, a lecture, and a discussion. In 1999 they presented *Pittsburgh in Vietnam.* The play addresses the issues of a soldier returning home after the war and his internment in a POW camp. The emotional and moving discussion that followed the play and the lecture was led by six veterans, and became a part of the center's oral history collection.

The Wheaton History Center's Kiebler Gallery, a space approximately twenty-four by fifteen feet, houses a faux slave cabin, designed, Alberta Adamson says, "as a knockdown that can be assembled off site. The program," Adamson explains,

> is divided into five stations: Capture in Africa and Passage to America; Control of the Enslaved and Law; Escape Stories; Life of the Enslaved with Secret Codes and Negro Spirituals; and Abolition with a recreated Underground Railroad Station. The Abolition station is always performed in first person. Life of the Enslaved is presented in costume in both first and third person depending if one of our African American interpreters is available. In all of the stations, the participants are involved with role-playing, such as seeing how you would fit into the small spaces on the ship from Africa, standing on an imaginary slave auction block, dressing up like Ellen Craft, who actually escaped by camouflaging herself as a white master, and singing a Negro spiritual containing hidden messages about when to escape. Authentic and reproduction slave artifacts are used in various stations: slave collar, shackles, dog collar, cargo crate used by Henry "Box" Brown to ship himself to freedom, and ship chains.

A second program, at the Wheaton History Center, *From the Homefront to the Battlefield: The Life of a Cavalry Soldier*, begins with a multimedia presentation as an introduction to the Civil War and the program. It contains four interactive stations with costumed interpreters performing in first person— Camp Life, Homefront, Chester and Jones, and Equestrian. At the Camp Life station students are "mustered," and can try on a wool uniform and be equipped with reproduction weapons and gear. At the Equestrian station they investigate the role and care of horses, with one of the interpreters occasionally bringing a horse to the program. The Chester and Jones station is brought to life by reenactors portraying the two captains. At the final, Homefront, station students learn what the war meant to those who stayed at home.

LaVoie states it well when she says that

> theatre can provide history museums with an effective tool for acknowledging individual experiences and encouraging personal reflection. Museum theatre can act as a vehicle to display individual stories, framing memories within a dramatic, engaging construct. Theatre can also serve as a catalyst to spark discussion, by providing an emotional element often missing from traditional

museum exhibits and programs. Particularly when created in conjunction with an exhibit or other supporting programs, theatre holds promise as a useful link between popular memory and public historical scholarship.

NOTES

1. LaVoie, "To Engage and Enlighten."

2. Peabody, "From Fact to Fiction: Creating Historical Drama," *Museum Theatre Journal* 1 (1993).

3. Peabody, "From Fact to Fiction."

4. LaVoie, "To Engage and Enlighten."

5. Jones, "Profile: Minnesota History Center," *Museum Theatre Journal* 3 (1995).

6. Pratt, "History Alive! Is in North Dakota," *Museum Theatre Journal* 4 (1996).

7. Williams, "Playing in the Stream of History: A Flexible Approach to First-Person Interpretation," *Museum Theatre Journal* 7 (1999).

8. Stillman, "Living History."

9. LaVoie, "To Engage and Enlighten."

Epilogue: The Future of Museum Theatre

On the first day of the first Theatre in Museums Workshop, a participant asked, "What made you think the world needed this?" It was not a friendly question, but then, he was not a friendly man. He had been told to attend the workshop by his manager and clearly did not wish to be there. Like many questions that sting, this one made us think. The answer to why many of us believe that theatre in museums benefits, if not the world at large, at least the worlds of theatre and museums, has been the subject of this book.

Art and science share the ability to challenge our easy perceptions of the world. As the poet Samuel Taylor Coleridge said, "The proper and immediate object of science is the acquirement, or communication, of truth; the proper and immediate object of poetry is the communication of immediate pleasure." The communication of immediate pleasure is a function of all the arts, not only poetry, and if we succeed in communicating a truth while giving pleasure, this is a worthy goal in itself.

Museums and the arts both face the challenge of having become primarily about entertainment. Few people would dispute that making learning fun is a good idea. But what happens when fun excludes critical thinking, self-discipline, and the raising of each student's self-expectations? During a time when educators are grappling with complex family and societal issues affecting them and their students, they are not to be blamed for seeing a visit to a theatre or a museum as an opportunity for recreation rather than learning.

E. Gordon Gee and Constance Bumgarner Gee wrote for the National Art Education Association that "the arts provide an opportunity to observe and form opinions and a context in which opinions can be informed and explored. As a record and reflection of our societal values, the arts provide a basis for us to ask the questions necessary to preserve civilization—questions involving issues and ethics, character and conflict."[1] Once more, the similarities between museums and the arts are striking. I would add that the strength of the arts lies in their ability to unleash our creativity, and that when that creative power is held in check, it becomes difficult to grow, to flourish, and to bloom.

The future of museum theatre depends on the value we place on the things theatre does best—touching our emotions, personalizing information, and challenging perceptions. It requires a commitment to imparting knowledge through people, rather than technology (ideally partnering with technology to the same end), and a willingness to take risks, to fail, and to succeed.

My countryman, writer Eduardo Galeano, said that "We are what we do, especially what we do to change what we are."[2] My own passion for theatre and education stems from a life experience that taught me that the fight for change, by which I mean compassionate improvement for all living beings, is a fight worth fighting even when it's lost, because the fight itself inspires others. When we strive for this kind of change, losing is not even a possibility.

In the twenty years I have spent in museums I have reached the by no means extraordinary conclusion that museums are in transition, which, as any mother knows, tends to be the most difficult stage of labor. In successfully transforming ourselves from places of static exhibitry to dynamic and interactive program spaces using the tools of both the education and entertainment industries, we have given birth to a demanding and challenging child.[3]

NOTES

1. Gee and Gee, *Arts Education for a Lifetime of Wonder* (Reston, VA: National Arts Education Association, 1997).

2. Galeano, *We Say No* (New York: Norton, 1992).

3. From an article by the author first printed in *Presence of Mind: Museums and the Spirit of Learning* (Washington, DC: American Association of Museums, 1999).

Appendix A:
Average Costs Incurred in Mounting Museum Theatre Productions

All costs depend on your individual needs, resources, and requirements. This list points out some of the possible expenses you need to consider.

THEATRE COORDINATOR

Runs every aspect of the theatre program, from hiring playwrights to supervising costuming. May also direct the shows. Depending on experience, this person will command a salary of between $28,000 and $55,000 a year, plus benefits.

DIRECTORS

Directors can be hired to a) direct only, or b) direct and produce. If they are only directing, it is *not* their responsibility to seek out, hire, or supervise the technical aspects of a production (e.g., costuming). Although the responsibility for the overall final product is theirs, they will expect someone else to do such jobs as prop gathering and the day-to-day supervision of the technical staff. Plan to pay a director a *minimum of $20 per hour*. A 20-minute monologue should not require over 20 hours of rehearsal.

If you hire a director/producer, then you need to state clearly at the outset that you expect him or her to oversee the day-to-day planning of the production. If necessary, the director/producer will interview and hire technical people, gather props, be responsible for setting up before and clearing after rehearsals, and run errands to collect set pieces or special effects materials. You should plan to pay a director/producer a *minimum of $25 per hour.*

ACTORS

Actors can be hired to (a) act only, or (b) act and help with technical aspects of the productions. If you hire actors only to perform, they will *not* be expected to set up for rehearsals, clean up after them, gather props, assist in set construction, or sew their own costumes. Their sole responsibility will be to attend rehearsals, learn their parts, and perform them. You should expect to pay actors *$9–$25 per hour,* or, depending on the number of performances they are being hired for, *$25–$75 per performance.* These rates can vary considerably if actors are on staff.

If you want actors to be their own stage managers, assisting in prop gathering and set construction, then you should expect to pay *$10–$35 per hour,* and *$50–$100 per performance.*

DESIGNERS (OF SETS, PROPS, AND COSTUMES)

Good designers—those who design what you ask for, deliver it on time, and do so within or under budget—are worth their weight in gold. They are as rare as directors who can also administrate. They also come in two categories: (a) those who design, and (b) those who design and build. In commercial theatre, the fees paid to designers vary from modest to princely. In museum theatre, the work is usually done on an hourly or a project basis. I recommend a project contract. The amount will be determined by the complexity of the design and the number of items required.

For example:

A production fact sheet for *The Road from Ban Vinai* reads as follows:

Summary of Play: A former pilot discusses his wartime experiences with the Hmong and reveals his son's decision to become a doctor in a refugee camp.

Setting: The Hmong House
No set required
Props: 1 map
1 easel
Costumes: Contemporary casual, for one actor

Material Production Costs:

Props	$ 50.00
Costume	$ 75.00
TOTAL	$125.00

Personnel Costs:

Playwright	$1,500	
Director/Producer	$ 500	20 hrs. × $25/hr.
Actor	$ 180	12 rehearsal hrs. × $15/hr.
	$ 300	20 hrs. research and memorization × $15
	$ 30	2 hrs. costume shopping × $15
	$ 500	10 performances × $50
TOTAL	$2,510	

The production fact sheet for *A Visit With Elizabeth Blackwell* reads:

Summary of Play: Elizabeth Blackwell, the first woman in the United States to receive an accredited medical degree, tells of her decision to study medicine, her numerous applications and eventual acceptance for medical training, and her struggles on behalf of women's health.

Setting: Science Live Theatre
  Set and props: early to mid-1800s period furniture
    and decor
  Costume: one day dress, 1830s

Material Production Costs:

Set materials	$500–$1,000
Props	$250–$ 500
Costume materials	$200–$ 300
TOTAL	$950–$1,800

Personnel Costs:

Playwright	$1,500	
Director	$ 300	15 hrs. × $20/hr.
Actress	$ 180	12 hrs. rehearsal × $15/hr.
	$ 300	20 hrs. memorization and research × $15
	$ 500	10 performances × $50
TOTAL	$2,780	

SAMPLE OVERALL YEARLY PROGRAM BUDGET FOR LARGE PROGRAM

Theatre coordinator's salary and benefits	$ 32,000–$ 50,000
5 actors' salaries and benefits	$150,000–$175,000
Set and props for 12 theatre pieces	$ 6,000–$ 10,000
Costumer and costumes	$ 12,000–$ 20,000
Playwright fees, or purchasing production rights	$ 5,000–$ 10,200
Incidental and miscellaneous expenses	$ 1,000–$ 5,000
TOTAL	$206,000–$270,200

This budget would enable you to mount approximately 12 scripts in one year, with the actors performing 4–6 times per day, 5 days a week.

Projected performances: 20–30 per week; 1,040–1,560 per year.

Per performance cost breakdown: $198–$157 per performance.

SAMPLE OVERALL YEARLY BUDGET FOR MEDIUM-SIZED PROGRAM

Theatre coordinator's part-time salary and benefits	$ 20,000–$ 30,000
3 part-time actors' salary and benefits	$ 80,000–$100,000
Set and props for 6 theatre pieces	$ 3,000–$ 5,000
Costumer and costumes	$ 6,000–$ 8,000
Playwright fees or purchasing production rights	$ 3,000–$ 6,000
Incidental and miscellaneous expenses	$ 500–$ 1,000
TOTAL	$112,500–$150,000

This budget would enable you to mount approximately 6 scripts in a year, with the actors performing 3–5 shows per day.

Projected performances: 15–25 per week; 780–1,300 per year.

Per performance cost breakdown: $144–$116.

SAMPLE OVERALL YEARLY BUDGET FOR SMALL PROGRAM

Theatre coordinator's part-time salary and benefits	$15,000–$20,000
2 actors' part-time salaries and benefits	$54,000–$60,000
Set and props for 3 theatre pieces	$ 500–$ 1,500
Costumer and costumes	$ 1,000–$ 3,000
Playwright fees or purchasing production rights	$ 1,500–$ 5,000
Incidental and miscellaneous expenses	$ 500–$ 1,000
TOTAL	$72,500–$90,500

This budget would enable you to mount approximately 3 scripts in a year, with actors performing 2–4 shows per day.

Projected performances: 10–20 per week; 520–1,040 per year

Per performance cost breakdown: $139–$87

Appendix B:
Elements of a Treatment

Audience	Demographics of the target audience: may include age, gender, or ethnicity
Length	Total running time of the play
Place Performed	Description and/or name of space: may include dimensions or particular characteristics
Setting	The place(s) where the play's events occur
Actors	Number of performers the play requires
Goals	One to three goals the play aims to meet. Goals should reflect the reasons for choosing this particular subject. Goals should begin with a verb, such as *to introduce, to demonstrate, to show*. It should be possible to measure whether or not goals have been met.
Content	A brief outline of the play's action.
Scenario	A description of the setting and why it was chosen. A description of the characters portrayed and their importance to the story.

SAMPLE TREATMENT

Science Museum of Minnesota
Script Treatment

Three Rivers Fantasy

AUDIENCE:	GENERAL (All ages should find something to enjoy.)
LENGTH:	30–45 minutes
PLACE PERFORMED:	Auditorium
SETTING:	THE IMAGINATION
ACTORS:	Four—three representing the Mississippi, the Minnesota, and the St. Croix rivers and one "every person" who will take on different "personae" as the play progresses.
GOALS:	1) To show how the rivers draw the natural world together into one tapestry and how we are a part of that threading together of the continuity of life.
	2) To demonstrate some of the effects both beneficial and detrimental of humankind on the rivers.
CONTENT:	You've heard of babbling brooks, murmuring streams, roaring oceans, but "Ol' Man River, he don't say nothin' . . . he just keeps rolling along." Well, it's time for the Mississippi and some of its tributaries to be heard. Water speaks to us, and when it can't any longer, we know it is in trouble, drying up, or too polluted.
	Each river has its own personality. The Minnesota River has always been a utilitarian/agrarian river. The St. Croix is perhaps more recreational, lighter natured. And then, of course, there is the Mississippi, the Big Muddy, the Granddaddy of Rivers.

SCENARIO: The play begins in a schoolroom represented by a desk, a student, and a back projection screen. On the screen is a series of slides or a video. A voice-over tape is of a teacher giving a lecture on rivers. The student is trying to pay attention but is soon swept up in a daydream. (A *CALVIN and HOBBES* type of daydream where the natural world takes over and comes to life.) The projection screen dissolves, the lights change to black light. Maybe a white glacier appears. Some parts of the teacher's lecture will come through the daydream. Perhaps he or she mentions how glaciers helped form the rivers. Soon the mighty Mississippi starts rising from the floor along with the Minnesota and the St. Croix. They will tell their own story. After all, rivers do have mouths. The student is swept along, and at various times becomes a character, such as: an explorer, a pirate, a lumberjack, a steamboat captain, or a farmer. Since this is a fantasy, birds, animals, and even inanimate objects might speak. The rivers speak of early times when a human footstep was rarely felt along their banks, and glory days when steamboats forged up and down them hauling cargo and passengers, and the forgotten days when railroads displaced riverboats, and modern times, when agricultural run-off and industrial pollutants have taken their toll. The rivers may form a trio and sing a song or two. But eventually the teacher draws the student from the daydream and back into the schoolroom, the rivers subside, the lights change, the projection screen reappears, and the fantasy ends. Or does it? There could still be another surprise.

Appendix C:
Contract for Services

CONTRACT FOR SERVICES

This Agreement is between ("the Museum") and _____
("Contractor") and is dated this _____ (day) day of _____
(month/year).

1. <u>Services</u>:

Contractor agrees to perform the following services for the Museum:

<u>Playwright</u>:

Contractor will research and write a _____ (length) play for
_____ (number of) actors following the specific subject matter and style
agreed upon in the approved Treatment. First draft will be delivered on
_____ (date).

Contractor will attend 2–3 rehearsals of the play.

Contractor will make all reasonable changes and rewrites to the script as requested by the Museum representative by _____ (date).

<u>Director</u>:

(Please refer to chapter 5 for ideas on how to describe the director's or direc-
tor/producer's responsibilities.)

Suggested language:

Contractor will attend auditions, select the cast, and conduct rehearsals according to the schedule outlined below. Contractor will attend _____ (number of) performances, and be available through _____ (date) to redirect the play as needed.

Contractor will plan and conduct auditions, select the cast, and conduct rehearsals according to the schedule outlined below. Contractor will attend _____ (number of) performances and be available through _____ (date) to redirect the play as needed. Contractor will also interview, hire, and supervise technical staff as agreed upon with the Museum. Contractor will negotiate script changes with the playwright and Museum representative.

Actor:

Contractor will attend rehearsals, memorize lines, attend costume fittings, and perform in accordance with the schedule laid out in Attachment A to this Contract.

Designers:

(Please refer to chapter 7 to determine the exact wording of this section for your particular project.)

2. Commencement and Completion:

Contractor will render these services between _____ and _____.

3. Review:

These services will be performed to the satisfaction of _____ ("Museum Representative"). The Museum Representative may request changes in these services as she may deem necessary. The Museum Representative shall determine the degree of completion of these services for payment as provided below.

4. Contract Sum:

The Museum agrees to pay the Contractor the flat fee of $_____.

5. <u>Special Conditions</u>:

Contractor understands that:

<u>Playwright</u>:

Copyright to be held jointly by the Museum and the Contractor.

Contractor to receive 25 percent of any proceeds received by the Museum for sale of the script.

<u>Actor</u>:

Contractor understands that special circumstances may require a change in the schedule (Attachment A). Contractor will inform the Museum in advance of any previous commitments that make changes difficult or impossible. The Museum agrees to give Contractor 24 hours notice of all changes to the schedule. Contractor will notify the Museum 24 hours in advance if for any reason he/she cannot meet the schedule. Contractor understands that full payment is due only for full adherence to the schedule. Any extensions to the performance dates will be negotiated under a separate contract or addendum.

Appendix D: Sample Position Description—Presenter

POSITION DESCRIPTION

Science Museum of Minnesota

TITLE: Presenter

DEPARTMENT: Public Programs

DIVISION: Museum Programs

REPORTS TO: Director of Public Programs

GENERAL DESCRIPTION

A full-time salaried position responsible for presenting demonstrations and theatre programs on topics and concepts in science and technology to the general public, stimulating creative problem solving, reflection, and action.

RESPONSIBILITIES

1. Perform science demonstrations and theatre programs for visitors and school groups. Including: set up and take down of sets, props, and seating; gathering audiences; and conducting postperformance discussions.

2. Stage manage, including: maintaining script and inventory updates; ordering and purchasing expendable materials; working with content specialists;

overseeing gathering of props; maintaining props by performing minor repairs using hand tools; notifying the director of Public Programs of breakages and/or needed replacements; working with exhibit designers and maintenance staff to maintain and update props; preparing space for rehearsals; scheduling and conducting line-throughs as needed or requested by director or other performers; conducting rehearsals in the absence of director; scheduling rehearsal space as requested by director.

3. Participate in rehearsals as assigned by director; memorize lines by first rehearsal.

4. Be informed and answer visitor questions about general museum information, programs, and activities.

5. Engage in ongoing reading and information collecting to assist in maintaining current scripts and facilitate postshow discussion with audiences.

6. Assist in training new presenters.

7. Conduct in-service annual theatre workshop by communicating with and instructing participants.

8. Maintain cleanliness of costumes and uniforms, perform minor repairs, and notify costumer of larger repairs.

9. Maintain handwritten daily audience attendance records.

10. Maintain updated office copy of personal work schedule.

11. Maintain desk, makeup table, and green room in orderly condition.

12. Attend all staff and Public Programs meetings as assigned.

13. Participate in evaluations of staff and audience response to presentations.

14. Participate in group script writing and rewriting process with fellow presenters, director, and/or playwright.

15. Transport, set up, and store sets, props, and costumes as needed for in-house maintenance. This could include lifting loads of up to 40 pounds and working off floor level on ladders, grids, or special sets.

16. Travel for, transport, set up, and perform outreach performances as assigned.

17. Assist with general light office duties.

QUALIFICATIONS

Presenter must demonstrate strong performance skills and have a demonstrated commitment to educational theatre; previous performing experience and formal training in theatre arts desired. Background and/or strong interest in science. Must have the ability to read, understand, and follow all reporting procedures.

ADDITIONAL PERIODIC DUTIES

- Write scripts.
- Train fellow staff members, volunteers, and youth in presentation skills.
- Direct youth groups, such as Magnet School and Projects Club, in defined theatre and demonstration projects.

ADDITIONAL ELEMENTS OF THE POSITION

- Work a flexible weekday, weekend, evening, and some holidays schedule.
- Interact with coworkers in a supportive, positive, and friendly manner. Maintain behavior patterns acceptable to coworkers and the general museum culture.

Appendix E:
Sample Audition Form

AUDITION FORM

Science Museum of Minnesota

NAME _____

ADDRESS _____

_____

TELEPHONE_____ (HOME) _____ (WORK)

Are you a member of Actors Equity? ☐ yes ☐ no AFTRA? ☐ yes ☐ no

Do you sing? ☐ yes ☐ well ☐ I can carry a tune ☐ with help ☐ no

Do you play any musical instruments? ☐ yes ☐ well ☐ haltingly
☐ I am taking lessons ☐ no

Can you read music? ☐ very well ☐ well ☐ yes ☐ no

Do you have any movement/dance experience? ☐ yes ☐ no
If yes, please detail: _____

_____

If you become a member of the Science Museum of Minnesota acting company, which production areas would you most enjoy assisting in:

☐ Costuming   ☐ Lighting   ☐ Sound   ☐ Writing   ☐ Research   ☐ Props

Do you know any foreign languages?   ☐ yes   ☐ no

If yes, which ones? _____

☐ "Tourist" level   ☐ I am fluent.   ☐ It is my native language.

Which area of the museum are you most interested in?

_____

_____

Do you have any immovable time commitments between _____
and _____?   ☐ yes   ☐ no

If yes, please give dates and times: _____

_____

Have you attached:

a) resume   ☐ yes   ☐ no

b) photograph   ☐ yes   ☐ no

c) references   ☐ yes   ☐ no

Appendix F: Sample Position Description— Theatre/Presentations Coordinator

POSITION DESCRIPTION

TITLE: Theatre/Presentations Coordinator

DEPARTMENT:

DIVISION:

REPORTS TO:

<u>GENERAL DESCRIPTION</u>

The theatre/presentations coordinator will be responsible for the overall co-ordination of museum theatre programs, productions, and special program events and projects that specifically pertain to theatrical productions.

<u>RESPONSIBILITIES</u>

- Work with curators and program specialists in planning, researching, developing, and implementing all theatre programs
- Supervise salaried, contract, volunteer, and intern theatre staff (i.e., actors, playwrights, directors, costumers, technicians) and serve as a liaison between the museum and other theatre production groups

- Coordinate planning and execution of technical program needs (sets, lights, props, special effects, etc.) with the appropriate personnel in _____ (list departments) or outside technicians

- Assist in the design of the overall program plan for existing and new exhibit halls

- Assist in locating and hiring appropriate talents for theatre programs, either through _____ (name of museum) or other organizations

- Prepare and supervise the implementation of theatre program and staff schedules

- Administer theatre program budget under the supervision of _____

- Assist in preparation of proposals for project funding

- Work with community groups and institutions to host guest performances and develop joint theatre projects as appropriate

QUALIFICATIONS/REQUIREMENTS

This job requires a person who both a) is a good manager and organizer, and b) has a solid background in all aspects of theatre. Specific requirements for these two aspects of the job include:

a) Managing and Organizing

- Demonstrated writing ability (required)

- Ability to supervise and work with people from varying backgrounds (required)

- Ability to work with detailed, accurate information such as schedules (required)

- Experience in budget preparation and administration (required)

- Proven ability to produce successful grant proposals (preferred)

b) Theatre Background

- B.A. in Theatre or equivalent work experience (required)

- Knowledge of all aspects of theatre production (required)

- Experience in directing (required)

- Experience in museum or educational theatre (preferred)
- Proposed Salary Range: $25,000–$45,000, dependent upon experience and qualifications

APPLICATION DEADLINE

All applicants must submit the following by _____ (date):

- Resume
- References
- Letter/statement of interest in position

Appendix G:
Glossary of Commonly Used Theatre Terms

Audition: A screening process for which actors prepare a short piece of their own choosing or read from the script.

Blocking: Actor's movements onstage.

Call: Refers to any appointment at a specific time. There are *rehearsal* calls, *costume* calls for fittings, *photo* calls for picture taking, and so on.

Callback: An invitation to audition again.

Choreographer: A designer of dances and complex movement sequences.

Costumes: Anything an actor wears onstage is considered a costume, whether it is a period garment or a T-shirt and jeans.

Cue: A directive for action or speech.

Dress rehearsal: A run-through with all technical elements, costumes, and makeup.

Flat: A covered framework.

Hand-prop: A small item handled or carried by an actor.

Musical director: A musical director teaches the actors their songs, sets the speed and timing of the music, and usually conducts the orchestra.

Plant: An actor placed in the audience and intended to pass as one of them.

Production meeting: A conference to share information.

Prompt book: A copy of the script with details of blocking, timing, action, set, props, and light cues.

Props: Any item onstage that is not listed as furniture or costume.

Sign-in: By half-hour every actor should have signed in. The stage manager then checks to see if anyone is missing and if understudies must be called.

Stage business: A specific action performed by an actor during the play.

Stage crew: Those who shift sets and props.

Stage positions: In the United States stage left is the actor's left; in Great Britain it is the director's.

Strike: The removal of a prop. A director may say, "Strike the candles from that table," meaning "Take the candles away." A stage manager may say, "Strike the act I set and set up for act II," meaning "Remove one set and set up another." When a play closes, the entire set is "struck," or removed from the theater.

Tech rehearsal: Technical rehearsals are for the people who run the lights and sound and move scenery and props. Actors walk through their parts.

Understudy: An understudy learns the part played by another actor and is ready to play that part if necessary.

Bibliography

American Association of Museums. *American Museums: The Belmont Report.* Washington, DC: American Association of Museums, 1969.

———. *Excellence and Equity: Education and the Public Dimension of Museums.* Washington, DC: American Association of Museums, 1991.

Anderson, Jay. *Time Machines: The World of Living History.* N.p.: American Association for State and Local History, 1984.

ASTC. *A Stage for Science: Dramatic Techniques at Science-Technology Centers.* Washington, DC: Association of Science-Technology Centers, 1979.

Breckenridge, Juliet. "The Heart Strings of Science." *Museum Theatre Journal* 9 (Fall/Winter 2000/2001).

Bridal, Tessa, and Susan McCormick, eds. *Science on Stage Anthology.* Washington, DC: Association of Science-Technology Centers, 1991.

Duganne, Carol Lynn. "Profile: Witte Museum." *Museum Theatre Journal* 3 (1995).

Forbes, Maggie. "Museum Theatre in a Children's Museum." *Journal of Museum Education* 15, no. 2 (Spring/Summer 1990).

Forest History Center's Staff Manual.

Franklin, Oliver. "The Large in the Small of It: How a Small Museum Uses Theatre to Enlarge Its Advantages." *Museum Theatre Journal* 4 (Spring 1996).

Galeano, Eduardo. *We Say No*. New York: Norton, 1992.

Gard, Larry. "Entertainment in Education: A Justification." *Museum Theatre Journal* 2 (1994).

Gee, E. Gordon, and Constance Bumgarner Gee. *Arts Education for a Lifetime of Wonder*. Reston, VA: National Arts Education Association, 1997.

Gonzalez, Cindi. "Museum Theatre Expands Texas Culture." *Museum Theatre Journal*, Spring 1995.

Grinell, Sheila, ed. *A Stage for Science: Dramatic Techniques at Science-Technology Centers*. Washington, DC: Association of Science-Technology Centers, 1979.

Hein, George E., and Mary Alexander. *Museums: Places of Learning*. American Association of Museums Education Committee Professional Practice Series. Washington, DC: American Association of Museums, 1988.

Hughes, Catherine. *Museum Theatre: Communicating with Visitors through Drama*. Westport, CT: Heinemann, 1998.

Indiana Historical Society. *Interpretive Master Plan*. Portland, OR: Formations, 1996.

Jones, Dale. "Museum Theatre and Evaluation: An Overview of What We Know." *Insights* (International Museum Theatre Alliance), Summer 2000.

Jones, Wendy. "Profile: Minnesota History Center." *Museum Theatre Journal* 3 (1995).

———. "Telling a Story That Is Not Your Own: The Manoomin Stories." *Museum Theatre Journal* 5 (Fall 1997).

Judd, Michael. "Interactive Interpretation: Puppetry in Museums." *Museum Theatre Journal*, April 1993.

Klein, Hans Joachim. "Exhibit Theater as an Interpretive Tool." Unpublished paper.

Koehser, David W. *Copyright and Publishing Law Update* (Minneapolis, MN, self-published newsletter) 8, no. 4 (2003).

LaVoie, Robin K. "To Engage and Enlighten: Theatre as an Interpretive Tool in History Museums." Master's thesis, Arizona State University, 2003.

Maloney, Laura, and Catherine Hughes, eds. *Case Studies in Museum, Zoo, and Aquarium Theater*. Washington, DC: American Association of Museums, 1999.

Miller, Douglas Stuart. "The Effect of Interpretive Theatre on Children in the Museum Setting." Master's thesis, Georgia Southern College, 1998.

Museum of Natural History. *AnthroNotes* (Smithsonian Institution) 24 (2003).

National Museum of Natural History. *Creating Exhibits: Policies and Practices of the Department of Public Programs.* Washington, DC: American Association of Museums, 1996.

Oestreicher, Lee. "Museum Theater: Coming of Age." *Journal of Museum Education* 15 (Spring/Summer 1990), 4–15.

———. "Museum Theatre: The Beginnings of a Natural Alliance." *Museum Theatre Journal,* September 1993.

Peabody, Ann F. "From Fact to Fiction: Creating Historical Drama." *Museum Theatre Journal* 1 (1993).

Pitman, Bonnie, ed. *Presence of Mind, Museums and the Spirit of Learning.* Washington, DC: American Association of Museums, 1999.

Powell, Corey S. *Discover, Science Acts Out.* N.p., 2000.

Powers, Jim, and Larry Roberson. "A Model for Collaboration." *Museum Theatre Journal* 3 (Spring 1995).

Pratt, Claudia M. "History Alive! Is in North Dakota." *Museum Theatre Journal* 4 (1996).

Rapkievian, Carolyn, and Johanna Gorelick, "Beyond the Thanksgiving Myth." *Museum Theatre Journal* 4 (Fall 1996).

Science Museum of Minnesota. *Theatre in Museums, Workshop Manuals.* St. Paul: Science Museum of Minnesota, 1984–2002.

Sellers, Charles Coleman. *Mr. Peale's Museum: Charles Peale and the First Popular Museum of Natural Science and Art.* New York: Norton, 1980.

Serkownek, Edith. "Museum Theatre: Its History and Practice." Master's thesis, Cooperstown Graduate Program, State University of New York, Oneonta, 1998.

Shively, Carol A. *Get Provoked: Applying Tilden's Principles. Legacy,* July/August 1995.

Short, Paul. "The Magic of Puppets: Suspending Belief." *Museum Theatre Journal,* Spring 1997.

Sommerfield, Bill. "George Washington Lives: The Art of First Person Interpretation Enriches Traditional History Lessons." *Museum Theatre Journal* 3 (Spring 1995).

Stillman, Diane Brandt. "Living History in an Art Museum." *Journal of Museum Education* 15, no. 2 (Spring/Summer 1990).

Sullivan, Robert. *New Traditions: Towards a New Museum Ethnography.* N.p., n.d.

Vincent, Catherine. "Bay on the Road: The Traveling Theatre Science Program of the National Aquarium of Baltimore." *Museum Theatre Journal* 5 (Fall 1997).

Williams, Bonnie. "Playing in the Stream of History: A Flexible Approach to First-Person Interpretation." *Museum Theatre Journal* 7 (1999).

Winslow, Lois. "Theater at the Pittsburgh Children's Museum." *Museum Theatre Journal,* 1994.

Wolsfeld, Susan. "Learning from Experience: The Only Rewrite Life Permits." *Museum Theatre Journal,* April 1993.

Zucker, Barbara Fleisher. "Anna Curtis Chandler: The Metropolitan's Costumed Storyteller." *Museum Theatre Journal,* Spring 1998.

Zweig, Bradley. "Profile: Theater at Please Touch Museum." *Museum Theatre Journal* 3 (1995).

JOURNALS

Arts Board News. Quarterly newsletter of the Minnesota State Arts Board.

Aviso. American Association of Museums newsletter.

Dimensions. Bimonthly news journal of the Association of Science-Technology Centers.

Insights. International Museum Theater alliance newsletter.

Journal of Museum Education. Published by Museum Education Roundtable.

MPR News. A bulletin published by the Museum Public Relations Committee of the International Council of Museums.

Museum News. November/December 1980, September/October 1990.

Museum Theatre Journal. American Association of Museums, Museum Theatre Professional Interest Council, 1992–2001.

Index

About the Author

Tessa Bridal has been working in the field of museum theatre for over twenty years. She is director of public programs for the Science Museum of Minnesota, one of the pioneer institutions in the use of theatre as an interpretive technique. Bridal has made numerous presentations at American Association of Museums (AAM) and Association of Science and Technology Centers (ASTC) annual meetings, served as a consultant for museums across North and South America, and written articles for professional journals and magazines. For a decade she chaired AAM's Museum Theatre Professional Interest Council, and she is currently an honorary board member of the International Museum Theatre Alliance. In 1994 AAM's Standing Professional Committee on Education honored Bridal with their Museum Educator's Award for Excellence for her "pioneering efforts in the use of theatre in museums and creating a nationally recognized model of educational programs."

Bridal, who was born and raised in Uruguay, is also a published novelist. Her book *The Tree of Red Stars* has won several literary awards, including the Milkweed Prize for Fiction, and was chosen by Random House Español as its first work of fiction for Latino readers, translated as *Las cinco puntas del lucero*.